Edexcel GCSE
History B
Schools History Project
The American West c1840–c1895
(Option 2B)

D0998033

Rosemary Rees
Series editor: Angela Leonard

A PEARSON COMPANY

Published by Pearson Education Limited, a company incorporated in England and Wales, having its registered office at Edinburgh Gate, Harlow, Essex, CM20 2JE. Registered company number: 872828

www.pearsonschoolsandfecolleges.co.uk

Edexcel is a registered trademark of Edexcel Limited

Text © Pearson Education Ltd 2009
First published 2009

This is a fully revised edition of *Longman History Project: The American West 1840–95*, by Rosemary Rees first published by Longman

13 12
10 9 8 7 6 5 4

British Library Cataloguing in Publication Data
A catalogue record for this book is available from the British Library

ISBN 978 1 846904 43 1

Edited by Florence Production Ltd
Typeset and illustrated by HL Studios, Long Hanborough, Oxford
Original illustrations © Pearson Education Limited 2009
Cover design by Pearson Education Limited
Picture research by Maria Joannou
Cover photo/illustration © Alamy Images/Brad Perks Lightscapes
Printed in Malaysia (CTP-VP)

Acknowledgements
The author and publisher would like to thank the following individuals and organisations for permission to reproduce material:

Photographs
AKG Images/National Museum of American Art p. 33; Alamy Images/Lordprice Collection p. 62; Alamy Images/North Wind Picture Archives pp. 10, 15, 19; Alamy Images/The London Art Archive/George Catlin p. 9; The Art Archive/Picture Desk/Buffalo Bill Historical Center, Cody, Wyoming pp. 2, 82, 104; The Art Archive/Picture Desk/Southwest Museum Pasadena/Laurie Platt Winfrey p. 82; The Bridgeman Art Library/Private Collection/Peter Newark American Pictures pp. 47, 50, 60, 69; The Bridgeman Art Library/Private Collection/Peter Newark Western Americana pp. 12, 13, 23, 24; Burton Historical Collection/Detroit Public Library p. 84; Corbis/Bettmann pp. 36, 40, 52, 87, 93; Getty Images/Photographer's Choice/Courtney Milne p. 6; Getty Images/The Bridgeman Art Library p. 48; Getty Images/The Bridgeman Art Library/George Catlin p. 7; iStockPhoto/Alex Slobodkin p. 102; iStockPhoto/Chris Schmidt p. 102; iStockPhoto/Efendi Kocakafa p. 102; iStockPhoto/Stockphoto4u p. 108; iStockPhoto/ZoneCreative p. 102; Library of Congress pp. 25, 37; Library of Congress/Currier & Ives p. 34; Mary Evans Picture Library p. 30; Roma Christensen p. 27; The Picture Desk/The Kobal Collection/20th Century Fox p. 64; The State of Missouri Historical Society p. 93; Smithsonian Institution/The National Anthropological Archives pp. 91, 92; Topham Picturepoint/The Granger Collection pp. 42, 59, 89, 97.

Written sources
Source A, p. 14 & Source E, p. 17, reprinted from Odie B. Faulk, *The Crimson Desert*, 1974, by permission of Oxford University Press, Inc; Source B, p. 37, reprinted from *The Sod House* by Cass G. Barns, published by the University of Nebraska Press; Source C, p. 37, reprinted from *Western Story: The Recollections of Charlie O'Kieffe, 1884–1898*, by permission of the University of Nebraska Press. © 1960 by the University of Nebraska Press. © renewed 1988 by the University of Nebraska Press; Source D, p. 38, reprinted from *Mollie: The Journal of Millie Dorsey Sanford*, by permission of the University of Nebraska Press. © 1959 by the University of Nebraska Press. © renewed 1987 by the University of Nebraska Press; Source H, p. 39, reprinted from *The Sod House* by Cass G. Barns, published by the University of Nebraska Press; Source E, p. 95, reprinted from Richard White *The Oxford History of the American West*, 1994, p. 249, by permission of Oxford University Press, Inc; Source B, p. 97, reprinted by permission of Henry Holt and Company, LLC.

Written sources have been freely adapted to make them more accessible for students.

Every effort has been made to contact copyright holders of material reproduced in this book.

Any omissions will be rectified in subsequent printings if notice is given to the publishers.

There are links to relevant websites in this book. In order to ensure that the links are up to date, that the links work, and that the sites are not inadvertently linked to sites that could be considered offensive, we have made the links available on the Heinemann website at www.heinemann.co.uk/hotlinks. When you access the site, the express code is 4431P.

Disclaimer
This material has been published on behalf of Edexcel and offers high-quality support for the delivery of Edexcel qualifications.
This does not mean that this material is essential to achieve any Edexcel qualification, nor does it mean that this is the only suitable material available to support any Edexcel qualification. Edexcel material will not be used verbatim in setting any Edexcel examination or assessment. Any resource lists produced by Edexcel shall include this and other appropriate resources.

Copies of official specifications for all Edexcel qualifications may be found on the Edexcel website: www.edexcel.com

Contents

Welcome to this Edexcel GCSE History B: Schools History Project Resource

Option 2B: The American West c1840–c1895

These resources have been written to fully support Edexcel's new GCSE History B: Schools History Project redeveloped specification. This specification has a focus on change and development through studies of societies in depth and of key themes over time. Written by experienced examiners and packed with exam tips and activities, the book includes lots of engaging features to enthuse students and provide the range of support needed to make teaching and learning a success for all ability levels.

Features of this book

- **Learning outcomes** structure learning at the start of each topic.

- **FASCINATING FACTS** give learning extra depth.

- **Key words** are highlighted and defined for easy reference.

- A topic **Summary** captures the main learning points.

- **Activities** Activities provide stimulating tasks for the classroom and homework.

How to use this book

Edexcel GCSE History B: Schools History Project The American West c1840–c1895 is divided into three sections that match the specification:

- Inhabitants and early settlers
- Development of the Plains
- Conflict on the Plains.

 A dedicated suite of revision resources for complete exam success. We've broken down the six stages of revision to ensure that you are prepared every step of the way.

 How to get into the perfect 'zone' for your revision.

 Tips and advice on how to effectively plan your revision.

 A checklist of things you should know, revision activities and practice exam questions at the end of each section plus additional exam practice at the end of the book.

 Last-minute advice for just before the exam.

 An overview of what you will have to do in the exam, plus a chance to see what a real exam paper will look like.

 What do you do after your exam? This section contains information on how to get your results and answers to frequently asked questions on what to do next.

ResultsPlus

These features are based on how students have performed in past exams. They are combined with expert advice and guidance from examiners to show you how to achieve better results.

There are four different types of ResultsPlus features throughout this book:

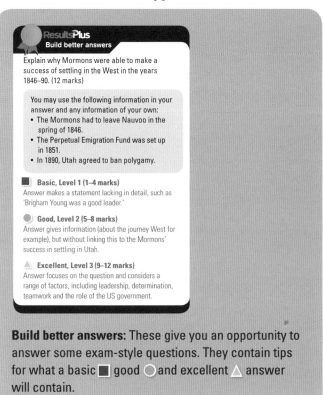

Build better answers: These give you an opportunity to answer some exam-style questions. They contain tips for what a basic ■ good ○ and excellent △ answer will contain.

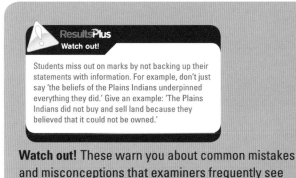

Watch out! These warn you about common mistakes and misconceptions that examiners frequently see students make. Make sure that you don't repeat them!

Top tip! These provide examiner advice and guidance to help improve your results.

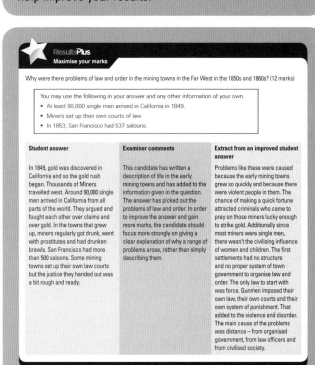

Maximise your marks: These are featured in the KnowZone. They include an exam-style question with a student answer, examiner comments and an improved answer so that you can see how to build a better response.

Inhabitants and early settlers

Introduction

The American War of Independence (1776–83) freed the American colonists from British rule. The United States consisted of just 13 states, strung out along the eastern seaboard. Parts of the rest of the continent were completely unknown to Europeans. Some of it was owned, or had been claimed, by the Spanish, French and British. Yet just over 50 years later, by a combination of good luck, force, treaties and money, the US government owned almost all of present-day America from the Canadian border to Mexico, and from the Atlantic to the Pacific coasts.

Aims and outcomes

By the end of this section, you should be able to describe, explain and understand:

- the culture of the Plains Indians and the ways in which they had adapted to living on the Great Plains
- the reasons for migration west and its dangers and difficulties
- the development of mining towns and the problems of law and order
- the problems faced by the **homesteaders** in settling on the Great Plains and the extent to which solutions were found
- changing attitudes to settlement on the Plains, the concept of **manifest destiny** and the role of the government.

*A Mandan Indian **medicine man**.*

FASCINATING FACT

When a Plains Indian child was born, the umbilical cord was dried. It was carefully kept in a tiny decorated case shaped like a turtle for a girl or a rattlesnake for a boy. The Indians believed that the cord that had given life to the baby would protect the child for the rest of their life.

However, owning the land was one thing; holding on to it was quite another. The US government believed that the only way to hold on to America was to fill it with loyal, white Americans. But there was a problem. The lands beyond the 13 states were not empty lands. The people who lived there were the native peoples of America – the North American Indians. These were people with very different hopes, ambitions, beliefs and lifestyles from the Americans who were to push the frontier of settlement westwards. Clashes, bitter and dramatic, between American settlers and American Indians were inevitable. The battleground was most frequently the Great Plains, as the new Americans first crossed them to settle in California and Oregon, and then, finally, settled on them to farm and make the land productive. This activity was totally alien to the Plains Indians, who had adapted to living on the Great Plains in a completely different way.

Activities

1 Work in pairs. Look at the painting of the Mandan Indian medicine man for exactly one minute. Cover the picture.

   (a) In two minutes write down everything you can remember about the painting.

   (b) Now swap your list with that of your partner and together look at the painting again. What did you both remember? What did only one of you remember? What didn't you remember? What did you get wrong?

   (c) What does this tell you about the impact the Mandan Indian medicine man had on you?

2 What do you think the medicine man intended his impact to be on other Indians in his tribe?

3 What does this tell you about Indian medicine?

claim an amount of land registered by a homesteader or miner for his own use

claim-jumping stealing another person's claim to prospect for gold in a specific place

counting coup the act of touching an enemy

Danites Mormon secret police

dry farming a technique whereby farmers ploughed their land whenever it rained or snowed, thus creating a layer of dust that trapped the moisture underneath

federal relating to a government that makes laws for all the United States

homesteader a person who settled on the Great Plains to farm the land

jerky strips of dried buffalo meat

manifest destiny the belief that white Americans should populate the United States from east to west coast

medicine man Indian holy man

mountain man a man who was a hunter, trapper and tracker in the Rocky Mountains

pemmican buffalo meat that has been pounded to a pulp, mixed with berries, poured into a skin container and sealed with fat

polygamy having more than one wife at the same time

primary settlement the first, most basic settlement

road agent highwayman

sacred land holy land

scalping cutting away the hair and scalp of a defeated enemy as a trophy of battle

sod house houses built from sods of earth by homesteaders

sod-buster another name for a homesteader

speculator person who bought land intending to sell it on at a higher price

sweat lodge a tipi where the air is heated inside and people go to sweat as part of a purification ritual

tipi the tent-like home of an Indian family

trading station the place where mountain men, Indians and traders met to buy and sell furs, skins and other goods

travois framework harnessed to a horse on which Plains Indians transported their belongings

vigilante a member of a community that took the law into their own hands

vision a person or object seen in a dream or a trance

1.1 The Plains Indians: their beliefs and way of life

Learning outcomes

By the end of this section you should be able to describe, explain and understand:

- the beliefs of the Plains Indians
- the way of life of the Plains Indians
- the importance of buffalo and horses to the Plains Indians
- the social structure of the tribes, and how and why they made war
- how the Plains Indians had adapted to living on the Great Plains.

Getting an overview

Indians believed that one Great Spirit ruled over the world. All natural things had spirits of their own and had to be treated with respect.

Plains Indians hunted buffalo. They were vitally important to the survival of the tribes. The Indians used every part of the buffalo they killed.

Plains Indians valued their horses above everything. They used horses to hunt buffalo, to move about the Plains, in war and for the sheer fun of riding.

All members of an Indian's family were important. Families lived in bands where most people were related to each other and could look after each other.

Indians did not need to keep law and order. Everything was ruled by custom and tradition. If Indians did anything wrong, they would be publicly shamed, which they hated.

Indians did not fight to conquer other tribes or to gain land. They made short, violent raids to steal horses or to kill men for revenge or honour.

Activities

Look at the overview panel on page 4. Each block describes a different aspect of the lives of the Plains Indians.

1 Which, for the Plains Indians, do you think was the most important aspect of their lives? Talk about this with a work partner and decide.

2 Now make the aspect you have chosen the centre of a spider diagram. Show how the other five aspects are linked to this and to each other.

3 What conclusions about the Indians' way of life on the Great Plains can you draw from your spider diagram?

Who were the Plains Indians?

Many different tribes made up the people we call the Plains Indians. Some tribes, such as the Sioux, were so large that they were called nations; others were much smaller. Although the tribes were different in appearance and had different languages and customs, they were all the same in that they had adapted to living on the Great Plains.

At the beginning of the 19th century, all the tribes had their own acknowledged territory on the Plains.

Some tribes were sworn enemies and would fight on sight. Others were traditional allies. Some made and broke alliances as conditions changed and in particular as white Americans began to venture on to the Great Plains.

Source A: Where the main American tribes lived.

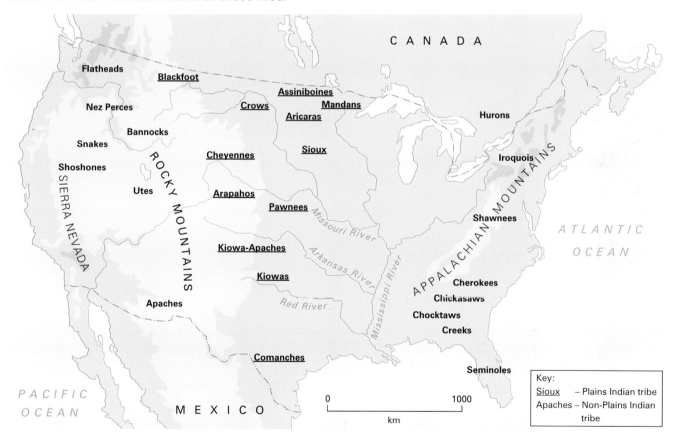

How religious were the Plains Indians?

The beliefs of the Plains Indians underpinned everything they did. Their belief in the unity of people and nature, and their profound conviction that humans should work with the power of nature and not try to tame it, influenced the ways in which they adapted to life on the Plains.

How important was the spirit world?

Indians believed in the Great Spirit, called Waken Tanka by the Sioux, who had created the world and who ruled over it.

As well as believing in one Great Spirit, the Plains Indians believed that all living things – animals, insects, fish, plants, birds and human beings – had spirits of their own that made them holy and deserving of respect. Even the rocks and streams had spirits. These spirits were very important because the Indians believed that the spirits could influence their lives and the way they lived on the Great Plains.

Other features of the natural world also had significance:

- Circles were important. Plains Indians believed that the power of the earth always moved and worked in circles. The circle of the horizon surrounded them; the circles of the sun and the moon were above them. The seasons formed one great circle, always coming back to where they started. Birds built round nests; the Indians' **tipis** were round and a circle of tipis made a village. Even the life of man was a circle, beginning with childhood and ending with the old behaving like children.
- Some land, particularly land in high places, was particularly special. This was **sacred land**. The Black Hills of Dakota, for example, were particularly sacred to the Sioux. It was to these hills that they took their dead for burial, and it was there that Sioux medicine men went for special guidance when there was an important decision for their tribe to make. Indians believed that they came from the earth and that, when they died, their bodies returned to the earth, like those of all living things. In this way all living things were part of the land and so the land could not be owned, or bought or sold. The land was part of life itself.

Source A: An Indian medicine wheel found in the Bighorn Mountains, Wyoming.

- It was through **visions** that Indians contacted the spirit world and the one Great Spirit that flowed through the universe. Boys and girls were given their adult name in ceremonies where they had their first vision. Boys fasted and prayed for several days alone, then told their vision in the **sweat lodge**. In some tribes girls fasted too, in others the coming of their first monthly period was celebrated.
- Dances were very important. Whole tribes could contact the spirit world through elaborate and sometimes agonising ceremonies such as the Sun Dance and the Buffalo Dance. For some Indian tribes, the most important ceremony of the year was the Sun Dance, led by the medicine men. By torturing themselves, Indians hoped to bring visions to themselves and their tribes, working with the spirits to make themselves better hunters or warriors and so bring glory to their tribes. In this way they would get guidance as to the correct course to follow, although they generally needed the medicine men to interpret the guidance given.

Source B: Black Elk, medicine man of the Oglala Sioux, describes a Sun Dance, in J. Neihardt, *Black Elk Speaks*, published in 1974.

> The next day the dancing began, and those who were going to take part were ready, for they had been fasting and purifying themselves in the sweat lodges and praying. First, their bodies were painted by the holy men. Then each would lay down beneath a tree as though he were dead, and the holy man would cut a place in his back or chest, so that a strip of rawhide, fastened to the top of a tree, could be pushed through the flesh and tied. Then the man would get up and dance to the drums, leaning on the rawhide strip as long as he could stand the pain or until the flesh tore.

How important were medicine men?

Look back to the picture of the Mandan medicine man on page 2. What did you decide about his impact on his tribe? Let's see if you were right!

The medicine man was important because he could interpret the visions of young men. He was important, too, because he could make contact with the spirits of all living things. Everything he did, from advising the chiefs whether it was the right time to go to war to curing the sick, stemmed from this. He was vital to the life of the tribe.

Sometimes, when there was great trouble – for example when the buffalo herds could not be found – the medicine man worked with the whole tribe to reach the spirit world and get guidance.

Source C: A Mandan Indian Buffalo Dance painted by George Catlin in the 1830s.

Medicine men also looked after their tribes in practical ways, as Source D shows.

Source D: Geronimo, an Apache medicine man, describes part of his work, in S.M. Barrett (ed.) *Geronimo: His Own Story*, published in 1974.

> The Indians knew what herbs to use for medicine, how to prepare them and how to give the medicine. This they had been taught at the beginning of time and each generation had men who were skilled in the art of healing. As much faith was held in prayer as in the actual effect of the medicine.

In reality, the active life of the Indians meant that they were generally fit and healthy. Their most common problems were: broken limbs and flesh wounds as a result of raiding and war; burns, bruises and grazes from buffalo hunting; fevers and rheumatism from being out in all weathers; and malnutrition when buffalo could not be found. The Plains Indians lived in small groups and were constantly on the move, so they did not suffer from the sort of health problems caused by, for example, the pollution of their water supply by human waste.

Indians believed that illness and accidents happened because they were possessed by evil spirits. It was, Indians believed, the job of their tribal medicine men to use the power that streamed through the universe to cure them of their ills, showing them how to work with, and not against, the spirit world.

Activities

1 How important to the Plains Indians was their belief in a spirit world?

2 Work in pairs. Make a list of all the things medicine men did. Decide which was the most important. Compare your ideas with others in your class. Can you reach an agreement on the overall importance of medicine men to their tribes?

3 How far would you agree with the painter and traveller George Catlin when he said that 'The Indian is a highly religious and moral being'?

For discussion

Plains Indians were skilled in tracking and hunting buffalo. Why, then, would they spend time taking part in a Buffalo Dance when they could be tracking down the missing buffalo herds?

How important were buffalo to the Plains Indians?

Life was not easy for the Plains Indians. They travelled long distances in freezing winters and scorching summers, either searching for, or following, the vast herds of buffalo on which their lives depended.

How did the Plains Indians hunt the buffalo?

Before they had horses, the Plains Indians stalked the buffalo on foot, covered in animal skins to disguise their human smell. Sometimes they stampeded a buffalo herd so that the animals were trapped in a valley or tumbled over a cliff. Horses made hunting much quicker and easier.

Source A: From George Grinnell *When the Buffalo Ran* published in 1920. Here he describes a buffalo hunt he watched. Grinnell was a white American, scientist, journalist, hunter and conservationist.

> Like an arrow from a bow each horse darted forward. What had been only a wild gallop became a mad race. Each rider hoped to be the first to reach the opposite ridge and turn the buffalo back into the valley. How swift those little ponies were and how admirably the Indians managed to get out of them all their speed! I had not gone more than halfway across the valley when I saw the leading Indians pass the head of the herd and begin to turn the buffalo. Back came the herd and I soon found myself in the midst of a throng of buffalo, horses and Indians. There was no yelling or shouting on the part of the men, but their stern, set faces, and the fierce gleam of their eyes, told of the fires of excitement that burned within them.

Source B: A buffalo chase painted by George Catlin in the 1830s.

What happened after the hunt?

When the hunters brought the dead buffalo back to camp, the women and children butchered it. They cut out the parts that were good to eat raw, such as the kidneys, liver and brain. The flesh was boiled or roasted. Anything left over was sliced into thin strips and smoked or dried in the sun. This **jerky** kept for a long time and would help feed the tribe during the cold winter months. The women also made **pemmican** from leftover meat. They pounded the meat into pulp, mixed it with berries and put it into skin containers. Then they poured hot grease and marrow fat over the containers to keep them airtight. Pemmican kept for a very long time without going rancid.

But it was not just the buffalo meat that the Indians used.

You can see from Source C that the Plains Indians used every part of the buffalo except one. This was the buffalo's heart. It was cut from the dead animal and left on the Plains. This, they believed, gave new life to the herd that had given the Indians so much.

Source C: Uses of the buffalo.

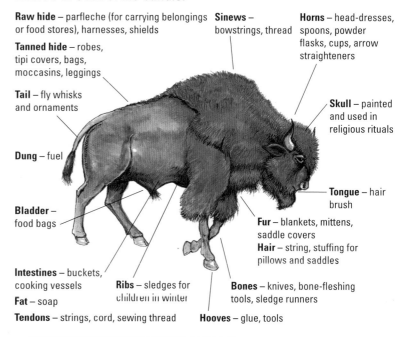

Raw hide – parfleche (for carrying belongings or food stores), harnesses, shields

Tanned hide – robes, tipi covers, bags, moccasins, leggings

Tail – fly whisks and ornaments

Dung – fuel

Bladder – food bags

Intestines – buckets, cooking vessels

Fat – soap

Tendons – strings, cord, sewing thread

Ribs – sledges for children in winter

Sinews – bowstrings, thread

Horns – head-dresses, spoons, powder flasks, cups, arrow straighteners

Skull – painted and used in religious rituals

Tongue – hair brush

Fur – blankets, mittens, saddle covers

Hair – string, stuffing for pillows and saddles

Bones – knives, bone-fleshing tools, sledge runners

Hooves – glue, tools

Activities

1 Study Sources A and B. Explain which source, in your opinion, provides the best description of a buffalo hunt.

2 A white American, Francis Parkman, spent some time living with the Oglala Sioux in the 1840s. When he returned home he wrote a book, *The Oregon Trail*. In it he said, 'When the buffalo are extinct, the Indian too must dwindle away.' Do you agree with him? Explain your answer.

For discussion

How far, in your opinion, does the Indians' treatment of the buffalo conflict with their religious views?

How important were horses to the Plains Indians?

For hundreds of years the Plains Indians were very poor tribes who made a living on the fringes of the Great Plains. They grew maize, ate berries and roots, and hunted buffalo on foot when they needed meat. Before them lay the Great Plains, bare and empty except for hundreds of miles of prairie grass and wild flowers and the roaming herds of wild buffalo. In spring and early summer the rivers, swollen by the melting snows, were deep and rapid; by summer they had dried up to a mere trickle. These Indians rarely ventured on to the Great Plains: survival would have been impossible.

So what happened to turn these people into proud chiefs and brave warriors, at ease living on the Great Plains? What made them ready and able to challenge the white Americans who came with their advanced technology and greed for land? The answer lies in one animal: the horse.

How did the Plains Indians get horses?

There were no horses in America until around the 1600s. The Spanish, who conquered the tribes living in Central America, built towns and farmed and bred horses there. They refused to sell horses to the Indians. Then, in 1640, the Pueblo Indians rose up against the Spanish. They drove the Spanish out and captured their horses. Keeping some for themselves for meat and for breeding, they sold the rest to other Indian tribes.

How did the Plains Indians use horses?

At first, Indians simply traded and stole horses. Gradually, they realised the horses' full potential. They used horses to hunt the buffalo, to help them transport their belongings when the tribe was on the move, in war and for the sheer fun and delight of riding hard and fast and performing feats of skill and daring. Horses transformed and dominated every aspect of their lives. Horses enabled Indian tribes to live on the Great Plains.

Source A: This woodcut by Frederic Remington shows a young Indian boy learning how to break in a pony. Remington worked in the 1880s as a cowboy and gold prospector. He travelled along the Oregon and Santa Fe trails and lived in Indian settlements.

Horses were so essential to the Indian way of life that, by about 1820, individual Indians were measuring their own wealth, and the wealth of their tribe, in horses. Status and prestige, too, were counted in horses.

Source B: The approximate number of horses belonging to the main tribes on the Great Plains.

Date	Tribe	Number of tipis	Number of Indians	Number of horses
1860	Blackfoot	300	2,400	2,400
1869	Comanche	300	2,538	7,614
1871	Crow	460	4,000	9,500
1871	Oglala and Brule Sioux	600	5,000	2,000
1871	Pawnee	260	2,364	1,050
1878	Hunkpapa/ Miniconjou Sioux	360	2,900	3,500

Activities

1 Look at Source B.

   (a) Which tribe was the largest?

   (b) Which tribe had the most horses?

   (c) For each tribe, work out the ratio of horses to Indians.

   (d) Which tribe was the richest?

2 How important were horses to the Plains Indians?

For discussion

Horses or buffalo – which were more important to the Plains Indians?

How did Indians solve the problems of living on the Great Plains?

Many different tribes, broken down into smaller bands, lived on the Great Plains, as you saw in Source A on page 5. It would be impossible to describe the lifestyles of all of them, so here we are concentrating mainly on the Sioux Indians. However, all the other tribes had solved the problems of living on the Great Plains in more or less the same way.

Indian homes

The tipi, sometimes called a lodge, was the home of each Indian family.

The tipi was an ideal design for a home on the Plains. It was basically a framework of wooden poles with between ten and twenty buffalo skins sewn and stretched over them. Look carefully at Source C. The flaps at the top of the tipi could be moved to direct the wind so that the smoke from the fire blew away. In summer the skins at the bottom were rolled up to let air flow through, and in winter earth was banked up around the tipi to keep it cosy inside. The conical design of the tipi meant that it was able to resist the strong winds that blew across the Plains.

Plains Indians were nomadic. The tipi could be taken down quickly when the tribe was on the move, and put up again just as quickly when they arrived at their new encampment.

Source C: This artist's impression of a tipi, cut away to reveal the inside, shows how an Indian family would have lived in it.

Source A: Colonel R.I. Dodge, a white man who travelled for many years among the Plains Indians, describes a tipi, in *Hunting Grounds of the Great West* published in 1877.

> In this small space are often crowded eight or ten persons, possibly of three or four different families. Since the cooking, eating, living and sleeping are all done in one room, it soon became incredibly filthy.

Source B: Chief Flying Hawk, of the Oglala Sioux, describes a tipi.

> The tipi is always clean, warm in winter and cool in summer.

Indians on the move

Plains Indians needed to be on the move, following the vast herds of buffalo that were essential for their survival. A tipi was an ideal home for people on the move. It could be taken down by the women (this was one of their responsibilities) in less than ten minutes. Two tipi poles attached to a horse formed **travois** that carried the family's belongings over the Plains to their next camp.

Source C: A painting of Sioux Indians moving camp, painted by Charles Russell. Between 1880 and 1892 Russell worked on cattle ranches and regularly sold drawings and paintings.

Indian children

Indians taught their children to respect all living things, including older members of their tribe. Parents prepared their children for their adult life. The boys learned the skills of horsemanship and fighting; the girls learned how to provide food and clothing for the family as well as how to deal with the tipi. Above all, they had to learn how to survive on the Great Plains.

All members of the family were important to each other. Since they lived in a band in which most people were related to each other, children were never without someone to look after them. Aunts and uncles looked after nephews and nieces, and cousins were treated like brothers and sisters. This was done not only out of love and kindness but to ensure that the band survived on the Plains. Children were the future of the band.

Source D: H.A. Boller, who spent eight years living among the Indians, wrote in 1868 about an incident he saw. This is part of what he wrote.

> A squaw with three small children was also left. She carried one on her back and another in her arms, while the eldest trotted along by her side. Some time after, a young Indian who had loitered behind came up and reported that the squaw had just killed the youngest because it was too small to travel.

Men and women

The job of the men was to defend the band against enemies, whether two-footed or four-footed. Once the band was safe, it was the women who, as you have seen, made day-to-day living possible. They were responsible for the tipi and all that that involved; for feeding and clothing their families; and for their family's possessions when they were on the move.

Not all marriages were happy. A Cheyenne man could divorce his wife by beating a drum and shouting, 'I throw her away'. In other tribes, a divorced man had to leave everything to his wife and go back to his mother's tipi with only the clothes he was wearing.

Widows and old people

Indians depended on the strength of the band not only to protect them against their enemies but also to survive on the Great Plains. They had to think of the safety and survival of the whole band as well as individuals within it. When men were killed out hunting or in war, their wives were shared out and married to the surviving men.

It was not unusual for Indian men to have more than one wife. In this way all the women were cared for and all women of child-bearing age had as many children as possible, thus strengthening the band. Old people, on the other hand, were a big problem for tribes and bands that were always on the move. The old people themselves usually came up with the solution.

Source E: George Catlin describes what happened when he was living with a Plains Indian family, in *Manners, Customs and Conditions of North American Indians* published in 1844.

> When we were about to start on our way from the village, my attention was directed to a very aged and emaciated man, who was to be left to starve. 'My children,' said he, 'it is necessary that you should all go to the country where you can get meat. My strength is no more, my days are nearly numbered, and I am a burden to my children. I cannot go and wish to die.'
>
> This cruel custom of leaving their aged people to die belongs to all the tribes who roam the plains, making severe marches, when such old people are totally unable to ride or walk.

Activities

1   Read Sources A and B. Why do you think they give such different opinions about tipis?
2   How did the tipi design solve the following problems facing Indians living on the Plains:
    • very little wood
    • extremes of temperature
    • strong winds
    • the need to move quickly and often.
3   What can you learn from Sources D and E about Plains Indians' attitudes to their children and to their band?

How was Indian society organised?

In order to survive on the Great Plains, it was essential that the different bands within a tribe worked together as they criss-crossed the Plains in search of buffalo. They also needed to support each other in times of trouble. All the different bands in a tribe would usually meet together in the summer for a great tribal camp, when the grass was rich

For discussion

Indians believed in the sanctity of all living things. How, then, can the events described in Sources D and E be explained?

13

enough to feed their horses and the Indians could kill all the buffalo they would need. As well as being social occasions, these were times when a tribe could work together to ensure its survival on the Plains. Some tribes, such as the Sioux, were part of a larger group called a nation.

Chiefs and councils

Chiefs led their band and were advised by their band's council. They themselves formed part of the tribe's council that advised the tribal chiefs. There was no system for choosing chiefs. They simply emerged as such because of their wisdom, leadership and spiritual powers or because of their skill as warriors or hunters. Chiefs were rarely chiefs for life. They came and went as their skills emerged and faded away.

No decision could be made until every man at the council, whether it was a band or a tribal council, had agreed to it. It was during council meetings that the ceremonial smoking of a pipe of peace took place. The Indians believed that the smoke from the pipe would carry their words and their desires up to the spirit world so that the spirits could help the members of the council make wise decisions.

Source A: A Sioux council, painted by George Catlin in 1847.

Warrior societies

Every tribe had its own warrior society, with its own special dress, dances and songs, and every man belonged to one. Members from the different bands in a tribe met to talk and exchange ideas. Warrior societies had different responsibilities in different tribes. Generally, their role was to protect women and children from attack and supervise the hunting, making sure that not too many buffalo were killed. The band council would always consult its warrior society before making a decision.

Source B: Colonel R. I. Dodge tries to explain how Indian society worked, in *Hunting Grounds of the West* published in 1877.

> Whatever the power of the Chief and the Council, there is another power to which both have to yield. This is the power of the hunters of the tribe, who form a sort of guild. Among the Cheyenne these men are called 'dog soldiers'.
>
> I cannot say exactly how the powers and duties of these governmental forms, ie chiefs, councils and dog soldiers, blend together. I have never met an Indian or a white man who could satisfactorily explain them. The result, however, is fairly good and seems well suited to the character, necessities and peculiarities of the Plains Indians.

Activities

1. Draw a flow chart or spider diagram to show how Indian society was organised.
2. Colonel Dodge (Source B) seems to think that the way in which Indian society was structured was sensible. Do you agree?

For discussion

How did the structure of Indian society help the tribes to survive on the Great Plains?

Why did Plains Indians fight?

Every young Indian boy dreamed of winning glory in battle. This was, for him, the only way to earn respect. He could enter a warrior society, maybe, or even gain a wife. By capturing horses and weapons, Plains Indians could become wealthy. Their chiefs used warfare as a way of testing their power and of increasing (or not!) their standing in their tribe or band.

Indians did not go to war to conquer others or to gain territory. They did not want to conquer others or gain land. Indians did not believe that anyone could own land, anyway (see page 4). Indian warfare was made up of short raids, made by small groups, in order to capture horses and weapons, or for revenge or honour. They had, too, to provide for their family and tribe on the sometimes hostile Great Plains. Dying in battle was not an option they chose.

What was the Indians' idea of bravery?

The Plains Indians would not have understood the way in which the white man fought battles. The white man was expected to stand and fight until the last person was dead. An Indian warrior did not want to die. What a waste that would be! Why risk being killed when you could slip away and live to fight another day?

For Indians, bravery was about facing up to responsibilities – being a good hunter and fighter, without taking unnecessary risks that could jeopardise one's life or the well-being of the tribe.

Source A: Odie B. Faulk, in his book *The Crimson Desert*, published in 1974, describes the Comanche Indians' idea of bravery.

> Their concept of bravery was completely different from that of the Europeans who came to live in the region. The Comanche thought it stupid to stand and fight when there was no chance of winning anything save honour. Instead they would slink away from such a contest, to return another day to steal horses, booty and captives.

Counting coup

Look carefully at Source B. What do you think is happening? It looks as though the Indian on the horse has killed, or is about to kill, the Indian on the ground. If you thought that, you would be wrong. Read Source E now and find out what was really happening.

Source B: Frederic Remington painted this picture of counting coup in the 1880s.

FREDERIC REMINGTON

Source C: E. A. Hobel wrote this in his book *The Cheyenne,* published in 1978.

War was transformed into a great game in which scoring against the enemy often took precedence over killing him. The scoring was in the counting of coup – touching or striking an enemy with hand or weapons. Coups counted within an enemy encampment ranked the highest of all. A man's rank as a warrior depended on two factors: his total 'score' in coups, and his ability to lead successful raids in which Cheyenne losses were low. Actual killing and scalping got their credit, too, but they did not rate as highly as the show-off deeds.

So **counting coup** – touching the enemy with his hand, or a specially decorated stick – was the greatest honour a warrior could win, particularly if his enemy was alive. The first man to touch an enemy in this way received the highest honour.

There were lesser honours for those who touched the enemy a second, third or fourth time.

Scalping

There was another reason for the Indians' desire to avoid death in battle – fear of being **scalped**. This was one of the worst things that could happen. If your enemy had your scalp, he had your spirit. So when an Indian killed a person in battle, he scalped the person and took the scalp back to camp.

Scalps were dried and displayed in many ways: on the top of tipi poles, hanging from horses' bridles, or sewn into the seams of warriors' clothing. The Plains Indians believed that if a warrior lost his scalp he could not live beyond death. So to scalp your enemy meant he would not be there in heaven to fight you.

Of course, if you lost your scalp, you would not be there either.

Activities

1 On a scale of 1–5, where 1 is the most difficult, rank these Indian customs that white explorers would find hard to understand:
   - attitude to land
   - idea of bravery
   - the Buffalo Dance
   - medicine men
   - attitude to old people.

2 To which did you give a score of 1? Explain why.

The Sioux Nation

Various Indian tribes have been mentioned in this chapter and you can see from the map (Source A on page 5) that there were a lot of them. The bigger groups such as the Sioux, as you have read, were called nations. Source D shows how the Sioux nation was divided into tribes and bands. Each individual tribe had a structure similar to the one shown for the Teton Sioux.

Source D: A diagram to show the structure of the Sioux Nation.

Challenge

Research a tribe!

Research ONE of the tribes that lived on the Great Plains. Find at least five features about your chosen tribe that shows how well they adapted to life on the Great Plains.

Share your findings with the rest of your class. In this way you will build up an invaluable class resource about the Plains Indians and the ways in which they worked with what they found on the Great Plains to build their lives there.

ResultsPlus
Watch out!

Students miss out on marks by not backing up their statements with information. For example, don't just say 'the beliefs of the Plains Indians underpinned everything they did.' Give an example: 'The Plains Indians did not buy and sell land because they believed that it could not be owned.'

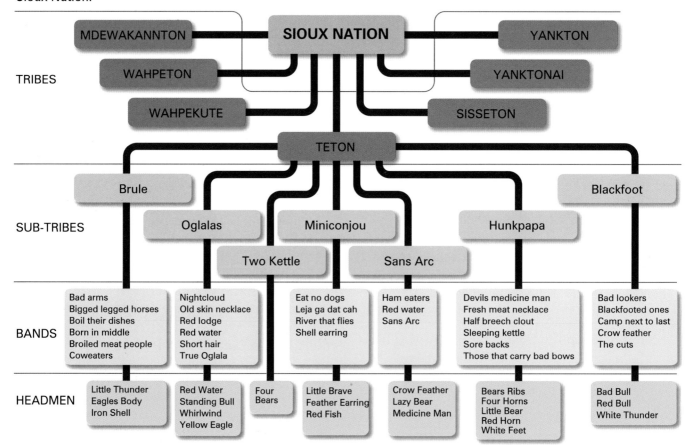

Source E: Odie B. Faulk, in his book *The Crimson Desert* published in 1974, explains the connection between counting coup and scalping.

> The Comanche warrior out to count coup had no wish to die in battle, for he had to guard his immortal soul. He wanted horses, he desired plunder, and he would take women and children captive if he could, but he did not want to die. To die in battle was to risk scalping, and a scalped warrior could not enter heaven. Courage was amongst the highest virtues amongst the Comanche, and they exhibited extraordinary courage when they carried off the bodies of their dead; but once a warrior's scalp had been taken, not even the bravest Comanche would touch the corpse.

Tribe vs. tribe

War between tribes usually happened in the summer, when the Plains Indians had built up their food supplies by hunting buffalo. Groups of Indian warriors formed raiding parties. What did they do? Why did they fight?

The Indians usually set out to steal horses from neighbouring tribes and bands. This could involve fighting and certainly involved counting coup. Indians also fought to protect their hunting grounds from tribes and bands that might have strayed there accidentally, or deliberately, in search of buffalo or antelope.

Many chiefs and elders welcomed warfare against other tribes. In war, they could exercise authority over younger braves, who were anxious to win honour and respect and could sometimes get out of control. Warfare was one way, too, of bringing all the bands together so that men, women and children could develop a sense of tribal unity and, again, acknowledge the power and control of the tribal chiefs.

For discussion

Why would some white people have thought Indian reasons for fighting very odd indeed?

Activities

3 (a) Put on the moccasins of a young Indian warrior, Raven Wing, and work with a partner, White Thunder. Together, make a list of the reasons why you desperately need to experience war. Put them in order of importance. Is your order the same as that of others in your class? If not, why not?

   (b) How far would a tribal chief's reasons for going to war be different from those of young warriors?

4 (a) In what ways was the Indians' idea of bravery different from those of white people?

   (b) Do you think this would lead to problems if they ever met in battle?

Summary

- Plains Indians believed in one Great Spirit that ruled over everything. All living things had their own spirits and had to be treated with respect because all life was holy.

- Land could not be bought and sold because no one owned it and some land was sacred. Through medicine men and visions, Indians could contact the spirit world and learn to work with it, making its power their own.

- Horses meant that the Indians could move onto the Plains instead of living on the fringes of them. They could move camp quickly, following and hunting the buffalo. Horses meant that Plains Indians could wage war efficiently and with speed.

- Buffalo were essential to the Plains Indians and meant they could live on the Great Plains. They used every part of the ones they killed to support their lifestyle.

- Tipis showed how well Indians adapted to living on the Plains: they used the materials available, housed extended families, were warm in winter and cool in summer. They could be taken down quickly – as the Indians needed to be able to follow the great buffalo herds – and could be easily transported by horses.

- The links between bands and tribes meant that tribes supported each other on the Great Plains, sometimes fighting against each other. In warfare, counting coup was more important than killing; this and scalping gave status to warriors.

1.2 Migrants and settlers in the West

Learning outcomes

By the end of this topic you should be able to describe, explain and understand:

- the reasons why different groups of migrants moved west
- the importance of the Californian gold rush and the impact of mining towns on the Great Plains
- the organisation and routes of the wagon trails and the dangers and difficulties of travelling west
- the long-term success of the Mormons in establishing a settlement at Salt Lake City.

Getting an overview

Here are some reasons why people chose to move west:

1837 Banks collapse in the East: thousands bankrupt

1839 20,000 unemployed people demonstrate in Philadelphia

1848 Gold discovered in California

1837 Wheat prices fall: Mississippi farmers face ruin

Mountain men tell of fertile land in California

Trappers tell of huge amounts of furs and fish in Oregon

1842 Act makes land in Oregon available cheaply

1837 Wages in the East cut by 40 per cent

1858–59 Gold discovered in Rocky Mountains

Missionaries want to convert Indians to Christianity

People do not pull up their roots and travel thousands of miles to a new life for no reason. For some, life where they are has become intolerable. These we call 'push' factors. For others, the main attraction lies in what the new life offers. These we call 'pull' factors. For many, the desire to move combines both push and pull factors.

Activities

1   Look at the reasons why people chose to move west. Which are the push factors and which are the pull factors? Divide them into two groups.

2   Which factors do you think were the most important: the push or the pull factors?

3   Think back to the work you did about the Plains Indians. How were they likely to react to the migrants crossing the Great Plains?

In this chapter you are going to look at four groups of people who travelled across the Great Plains:

- trappers and mountain men
- settlers heading for Oregon and California
- miners
- Mormons.

As you work through this chapter, think about three things:

- Did they all go west for the same reason?'
- Did they all experience the same problems?
- What impact did they have on the Indians who roamed the Great Plains?

Why were mountain men and trappers important?

Mountain men and fur trappers were vital to the development of the American West. The fur trappers were the first white men to cross the Great Plains and the Rocky Mountains, trapping beaver and hunting antelope and other animals for their fur. Some worked for companies that sold the fur to fashion houses in the eastern states and in Europe, where fur hats were hugely popular. Many of them were completely independent, calling themselves mountain men, spending all their lives roaming the Rockies and Sierra Nevada, selling skins and furs to traders when they could. They found routes through the Rockies and Sierra Nevada that had previously been known only to Indians. They saw, beyond the mountain ranges, the rich, fertile lands of Oregon and California. And they talked about what they saw.

Mountain men and Indians: friends or foes?

Source A: *I took ye for an Injun,* painted by Frederic Remington in 1890.

"I TOOK YE FOR AN INJIN."

It is easy to see why Frederic Remington called his painting of two mountain men *I took ye for an Injun*. Mountain men, like Indians, were expert trackers and hunters and knew the ways of animals and the uses of plants. Sometimes they worked with Indians and sometimes they fought them. Some Indian nations, such as the Blackfoot, were dangerous enemies. Others, such as the Shoshone, were friendlier, and many mountain men married Indian women. One mountain man, Jim Bridger, had three Indian wives in succession, and another, Jim Beckwith, even became an Indian chief. Jeremiah Johnson, on the other hand, killed every Indian he came across. This was, he said, because an Indian had scalped and killed his pregnant wife.

While some mountain men may have brought comfort and support to some Indians, in general the Indians gained little from them. Along with the mountain men came firearms, alcohol, smallpox and sexually transmitted diseases – and the beginning of the destruction of the Indian way of life.

Mountain men and the government: friends or foes?

Government explorers were in the Rockies and the Sierra Nevada to map and chart, not to hunt. Their interests did not clash with those of the mountain men who were there to hunt and trap, and so usually any help they could give each other was welcomed. For example, in 1842 John Charles Fremont and the US Army Corps of Topographical Engineers began a survey of the Rocky Mountains. Mountain man Joseph Walker, using his specialised knowledge, helped guide the expedition.

Source B: From an account written by an army surveyor who was sent to the West in the 1840s to map it scientifically.

> Jim Bridger is one of the hardy race of mountain men who are now disappearing from the continent, being enclosed in a wave of civilisation. With a buffalo skin and a piece of charcoal he will map out any portion of this immense region, and draw mountains, streams and the circular valleys called 'holes' with wonderful accuracy.

Source C: An Englishman, George Ruxton, lived among the mountain men in 1847 and wrote in 1849 about their importance in opening up the way to the West.

> Every hole and corner in the vast wilderness of the 'Far West' has been explored by these hardy men. From the Mississippi to the mouth of the Colorado in the west, from the frozen regions of the north to Mexico in the south, the beaver-hunter has set his traps in every creek and stream. All this vast country, but for the daring enterprise of these men, would even now be an unknown land to geographers, as indeed a great portion still is in 1849.

19

Jim Bridger: an important mountain man

In 1822, Jim Bridger joined General William Ashley's Upper Missouri Expedition and explored the Yellowstone region. This gave him a taste for exploring and for the roaming life of a mountain man. In 1824, on a beaver-hunting expedition, he became the first white man to see the Great Salt Lake. Six years later, with several other mountain men, he bought the Rocky Mountain Fur Company, and when the fur trade collapsed in the early 1840s he moved on to build a trading post, Fort Bridger, to provide supplies for migrants on the Oregon Trail.

Bridger led hundreds of wagon trains safely through the Rockies. In 1850, looking for a better way through, he discovered a pass that was later named after him and which shortened the Oregon Trail by 61 miles. Years later, the Bridger Pass was the chosen route for the Union Pacific Railroad and Interstate 80. In 1864, he created the Bridger Trail, which was an alternative route from Wyoming to the gold fields of Montana that avoided the dangerous Bozeman Trail. He worked as a guide and army scout during the first Powder River Expedition against the Sioux and Cheyenne who were blocking the Bozeman Trail (Red Cloud's War) and was discharged from the army in 1865. Blind, and suffering from arthritis and rheumatism, he died on his farm near Kansas City, Missouri, in 1881.

Buying, selling and gossiping

The big companies, such as the American Fur Company, built **trading stations** where their agents could buy fur and skins from the trappers and mountain men. These trading stations were called 'forts' because they could be defended against attack from hostile Indians. News of rich farming land west of the Rocky Mountains was brought by traders travelling up and down the Mississippi and Missouri rivers and spread eastwards to farmers in Ohio and Illinois. It was news that was to change the lives of thousands of people.

For discussion

Do you agree that Jim Bridger prepared the way for the settlement of the West?

Activities

1 In what ways was the life of a mountain man similar to that of a Plains Indian?

2 Look back at Source A on page 19. We know what Frederic Remington thinks they are saying to each other, but how does the conversation continue? Are they swapping information about the best places to trade their furs and skins? Are they talking about hostile or friendly Indians? With a partner, work out the conversation and make it as realistic as you can. You could record it – or argue it out in front of your class.

Wagon trains westward!

Look back at the work you did on page 18 and at the 'push' and 'pull' factors. Focus on the 'push' factors you identified.

- The economic depression that hit the USA in 1837, with banks in the East crashing, led to thousands losing their savings, wages being cut by 40 per cent and unemployment soaring.
- In the Midwest, farmers faced ruin because the price of the corn they grew collapsed.
- Farmers in the Mississippi valley were beginning to feel crowded in. The population of Missouri, for example, grew from 14,000 in 1830 to 353,000 in 1840.

Add to this the knowledge that mountain men such as Jim Bridger were willing to act as guides through the Rockies and Sierra Nevada, and it is not surprising that thousands of men, women and children deserted their homes in the East for what they thought would be a better, or certainly not a worse, life in the West.

The earliest migrants

In the early days, the first migrants found their own way west. After two unsuccessful attempts to get wagons over the Sierra Nevada in 1841 and 1842, the first wagons arrived in Oregon in 1843. The following year, the first wagons arrived in California.

Source A: Routes to the West: what was it like to travel West in the 1840s?

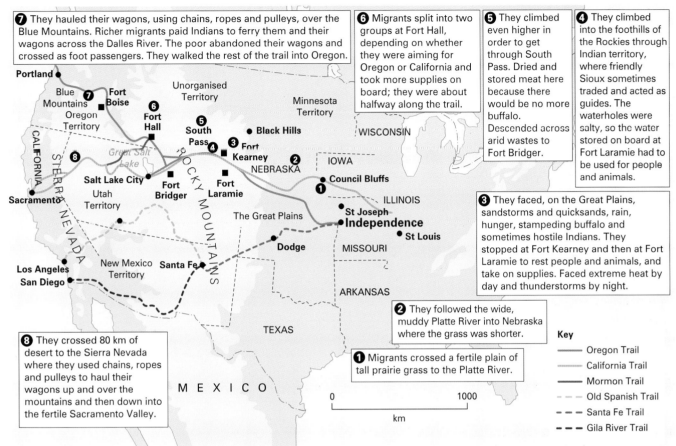

7 They hauled their wagons, using chains, ropes and pulleys, over the Blue Mountains. Richer migrants paid Indians to ferry them and their wagons across the Dalles River. The poor abandoned their wagons and crossed as foot passengers. They walked the rest of the trail into Oregon.

6 Migrants split into two groups at Fort Hall, depending on whether they were aiming for Oregon or California and took more supplies on board; they were about halfway along the trail.

5 They climbed even higher in order to get through South Pass. Dried and stored meat here because there would be no more buffalo. Descended across arid wastes to Fort Bridger.

4 They climbed into the foothills of the Rockies through Indian territory, where friendly Sioux sometimes traded and acted as guides. The waterholes were salty, so the water stored on board at Fort Laramie had to be used for people and animals.

3 They faced, on the Great Plains, sandstorms and quicksands, rain, hunger, stampeding buffalo and sometimes hostile Indians. They stopped at Fort Kearney and then at Fort Laramie to rest people and animals, and take on supplies. Faced extreme heat by day and thunderstorms by night.

2 They followed the wide, muddy Platte River into Nebraska where the grass was shorter.

1 Migrants crossed a fertile plain of tall prairie grass to the Platte River.

8 They crossed 80 km of desert to the Sierra Nevada where they used chains, ropes and pulleys to haul their wagons up and over the mountains and then down into the fertile Sacramento Valley.

Key
— Oregon Trail
— California Trail
— Mormon Trail
– – – Old Spanish Trail
– ■ – Santa Fe Trail
– ▪ – Gila River Trail

0 ———— 1000
km

Before long there were several tried and trusted trails that were safe enough, most of the time, for migrants to use without the help of guides. The most popular trails were the California Trail and the Oregon Trail. The route to California was 3,800 km long and took from April to November, or even December. The route to Oregon took longer.

These routes became well known but this did not mean that they were easy or even safe. According to official estimates, 34,000 people died on the westward trails between 1840 and 1860.

How did people prepare for and make the journey west?

Independence, a town on the border of Missouri, was important to the first migrants. Here they gathered before beginning the trek across the Great Plains and the long haul up and over the Rocky Mountains and the Sierra Nevada. They checked supplies and waited until there were sufficient wagons to make up a large-sized wagon train because it was dangerous to travel alone.

It was important to travel with people with a variety of useful skills, and some people waited for many days before they were happy with the migrants with whom they were travelling. No one, for example, would want to travel without someone capable of hunting. They waited, too, until the prairie grass was rich and sweet enough to feed the animals.

Most wagon trains ended up with at least 20 wagons and some had many more. One of the largest left Independence in 1843 with a thousand men, women and children.

The Donner Party: death and disaster in 1846

Some 60 wagons and 300 migrants, led by the wealthy brothers Jacob and George Donner, left Independence in May 1846. Despite having more women, elderly people and children than was usual and few of the skills that would be needed during the trek, they were very well equipped, and common sense should have seen them through. So what went wrong?

Source B: Extracts from diaries kept by migrants as they travelled the trails westward.

- But another enemy, unseen and without one audible word of demand or threat, was that very hour advancing upon us, and made our wagon his first point of attack. That enemy was cholera. (Unknown author)
- The hem of my dress caught on an axle-handle, sending me under the wheels, both of which passed over me, badly crushing my left leg before father could stop the oxen. (Catherine Sagar 1844)
- May 1: Took an hour to build a fire this morning, the ground was very wet and the wind blew cold from the north-west. August 13: We came to a stopped wagon. We saw the bodies of three dead men. They had been dead two or three weeks. One had his head and face cut out, another his legs, a third his hands and arms. (Jane Gould 1862)

A leaflet produced by a trail guide, Lansford Hastings, had impressed the Donner brothers. He claimed to have found a short cut to California. This new trail left the traditional one at Fort Bridger and curved south-west below the Great Salt Lake before joining the traditional trail again. What the migrants did not know was that he had not used the short cut himself – he simply thought it should work.

The Donner party argued furiously about whether or not to take the short cut and the group split. The larger part intended to follow the traditional trail, and a smaller group of about 80, including the Donner brothers, intended to take Hastings's short cut.

At Fort Bridger the Donners led their party south-west, trying to follow what they believed was a short cut through Utah into Nevada. They suffered badly in the desert, losing four wagons and 300 head of cattle; they had quarrelled among themselves and one man had killed another. By the time the Donner party reached the Sierra Nevada, they were late, badly demoralised and had little food.

Worse was to come. In 1846 the snows came early, and October found the Donner party trapped in deep snow on the wrong side of the Sierra Nevada

without the strength to carry on. They decided to dig in for the winter. Conditions quickly became appalling. Icy blizzards howled around them; animals died; food stocks dwindled; the first migrant died of starvation on 15 December. No one in the party had the skill to hunt in the harsh Sierra environment.

A small group of fifteen adults, eight men, five women and two Indian guides decided to try to battle through drifts and blizzards on foot to California to get help. The small amount of food they took with them quickly ran out. Four of the men were frozen to death in a snowstorm. Their companions roasted and ate them, packing the leftover food for future meals, and labelling it so that no one ate their husband or wife. The Indians refused to eat human flesh, so after two days they were shot, butchered and eaten. Finally, on 10 January, the remaining nine adults stumbled into Johnson's Ranch and pleaded for help. It had taken them 32 days.

Word quickly spread, and a rescue operation began to try to reach the trapped Donner party. Four separate parties set out from California, risking their own lives as they carried vital supplies into the treacherous Sierra Nevada. They found what was left of the Donner party. Half were dead and those who were left had survived by eating their dead friends and relatives.

Source C: Captain Fellun, who led one of the rescue parties, described what he found when he reached the Donner party.

A horrible scene presented itself. Human bodies terribly mutilated, legs, arms and skulls scattered in every direction. At the mouth of a tent stood a large pot, filled with human flesh cut up. It was the body of George Donner. His head had been split open and the brains extracted.

For discussion

Who was to blame for the Donner party's failure?

Activities

1 Why did some people decide to leave all that they knew and loved, and travel west as migrants?

2 Work with a partner. Create a handbook of advice for people intending to travel west in the wagon trains. Use all the information in this section to make it really helpful – and better than Lansford Hastings's leaflet seems to have been!

3 What was the key point that turned the Donner party's expedition into a disaster?

ResultsPlus
Build better answers

Describe the problems faced by migrants travelling west by wagon to Oregon and California. (9 marks)

 Basic, Level 1 (1–3 marks)
Answer makes undeveloped comments about the journey being difficult or gives one unspecific example such as 'it was very tricky getting over the Rocky Mountains'.

 Good, Level 2 (4–6 marks)
Answer describes the difficulties, giving details, for example, 'emigrants going to Oregon had to use ropes, chains and pulleys to haul their wagons over the Blue Mountains'.

 Excellent, Level 3 (7–9 marks)
Answer explains the problems, adding detail in support. For example, showing the problems caused by severe weather, unknown territory and difficult terrain and illustrating these points using the Donner party's experience.

Miners: the wrong sort of migrant?

The early migrants made the long, dangerous trek westwards in search of a better life for themselves and their families. There was, however, another group of people travelling west to California. They were not travelling with their families and they were not intending to settle down.

Gold rush!

Early in 1848, gold was accidentally discovered in California. Quickly the news reached the eastern states and then the rest of the world. Within months, 40,000 men were reported to be crossing the Great Plains and 60 ships carrying would-be gold miners left ports in America and Europe, bound for California. Many of the men were not miners at all. They simply wanted to get rich quickly. By the end of 1848, around 10,000 men were digging for gold in California; by the end of 1849, there were 90,000 gold-miners there – nicknamed the 'forty-niners'. Most of them did not find gold and wandered back home or drifted from mine to mine. Some, however, did strike gold and became extremely rich indeed. It was stories of these lucky strikes that kept men going.

Gradually the gold in California, which was near the surface and easy to mine, was exhausted. The days of the 'forty-niners' were over and they began the weary journey home. Then, in 1858–59, gold was discovered in the Pikes Peak region of the Rocky Mountains, in Idaho (1860), in Montana (1862), in Arizona (1863) and in the Black Hills of Dakota (1874). This last discovery led to gold prospectors swarming all over the Sioux's hallowed ground, with devastating results (see pages 80–82).

Source A: A contemporary painting of men panning for gold during the Californian gold rush of 1849. This was the simplest way of looking for gold – sieving dirt from a river bed, hoping that what remained in the sieve would have that telltale gleam of gold.

Miners and mining towns

The early miners had to live somewhere, and hundreds of shanty towns sprung up, only to vanish when the gold ran out and the miners moved on. These **primary settlements** were often little more than groups of filthy shacks beside a dust road. Dysentery, scurvy and typhoid were common, and there were even occasional outbreaks of cholera. It is hardly surprising that, when they were not working, the miners took themselves off to local saloons. San Francisco in 1853, for example, had as many as 537 saloons, where miners could drink and gamble all day and where some prostitutes charged as much as $400 a night.

By the mid-1850s, the surface gold in California was almost exhausted, the 'forty-niners' were leaving and the professional miners moved in. Many of these had worked in the tin and gold mines of Cornwall, and were able to sink and work deep mines. They were backed by businessmen working in the east coast states of the USA, who put money into machinery and mills, and in doing so turned gold mining into a profitable industry. These professional miners built and lived in permanent mining towns, and brought their wives and families with them.

How was law and order kept in the mining towns?

The early mining towns were tough, lawless places, run by the men with the fastest guns, where violence was commonplace. **Claim-jumping** – stealing one man's **claim** to a mine after gold had been discovered there – was the most common crime and often led to murder. Far from **federal** law officers and lacking state law, the miners set up their own courts, which dispensed rough justice and were often corrupt.

When the professional miners moved in with their families and the towns became permanent, the system of management of law and order became more formalised. Town meetings chose a chairman and officers; claims to mines had to be recorded; sheriffs were appointed to arrest criminals and a court of miners decided on guilt or innocence and punishments. However, trials were quick, and justice was rarely fair; punishments were usually

Source B: A poster of 1865 advertising travel by steamboat and wagon from the Missouri River to the gold mines of Idaho.

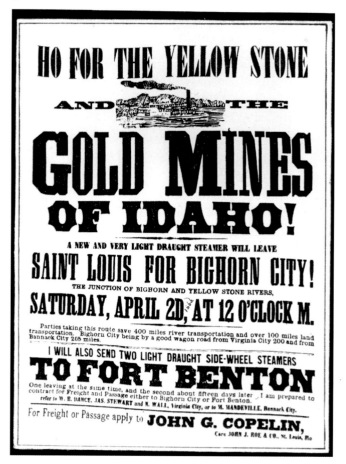

flogging, banishment or hanging. Sometimes, however, the courts could not cope with the level of lawlessness. Ordinary citizens began setting up vigilance committees who took the law into their own hands. These **vigilantes** held instant trials, after which many a condemned man would be seen hanging from a nearby tree, guilty or not.

There were times when this worked well. In the 1860s, the people of Bannack, Montana, were terrorised by a well-organised gang of about 100 **road agents**. It gradually became clear that Henry Plummer, the elected sheriff and a well-respected member of the community, was the leader of the gang. A vigilance committee was set up, and one of the gang confessed. Plummer was caught and hanged by the vigilantes in 1864.

However, before long, people in the townships began to fear the vigilantes themselves. It was all too easy to execute someone who had got on the wrong side of an influential citizen.

What was the impact of the discovery of gold in the West?

The discovery of gold had a profound effect, not only on the regions where it was found but on the economic development of the USA as a whole:

- It increased the supply of money and encouraged investment in the mining industry and industry.
- It stimulated the rapid growth of San Francisco as a financial centre.
- It ensured that when a railroad was built across America in the 1860s, it went to California, not Oregon.
- The wealth created gave the USA a leading role in world trade.
- It stimulated the movement west in the 1850s.

But there were problems:

- The influx of gold prospectors from around the world led to racial conflict, with American workers often refusing to work with Chinese miners.
- Taxes were imposed on foreign miners, which led to resentment.
- Indians in California were virtually wiped out.

Activities

1 How far do you think Source B acted as a good 'pull' factor to entice people to move westwards?

2 You are a journalist on an east-coast newspaper. Your editor has sent you on a 'fact-finding' mission to the mining towns of the West and he wants a hard-hitting article from you. Write that article – along with the headlines!

For discussion

Did the discovery of gold affect the development of the American West for good or for ill?

The Mormons: a successful group of migrants?

Today, Salt Lake City in the state of Utah is one of the most prosperous cities in the USA. The story behind the founding of this city is one of determination, religious conviction and persecution, coupled with the extraordinary leadership of Joseph Smith and Brigham Young.

Joseph Smith and the first Mormons (1823–31)

Joseph Smith, the son of a poor farmer from Vermont, claimed that in 1823 he dug up some golden plates from a mountainside in Palmyra, New York State. He said he had been guided to the plates by an angel, Moroni, who helped him translate the mysterious writing on them. It said that whoever found the plates would restore the church of Jesus Christ in America and build up God's kingdom on earth ready for Christ's second coming. Joseph Smith was that man.

Joseph Smith started with only five followers, who were called Mormons, but by 1830 his charismatic public speaking resulted in several hundred people joining his Church of Latter Day Saints. Whilst Mormonism was rooted in Christian beliefs, they had several different ideas including polygamy where a man could marry several wives at once. They became very unpopular in New York State. Preachers denounced them as blasphemous, and newspapers accused Joseph Smith of being a fraudster; mobs attacked his house and Mormons were shot at in the street. After praying for guidance, Joseph Smith took his followers to the village of Kirtland, Ohio. But, as you will see, the Mormons were not able to stay in Ohio, nor were they able to stay in Missouri or Illinois.

Source A: An American cartoon from the 1840s, making fun of polygamy.

Mormons on the Move

Ohio 1831–37

What did the Mormons do?	How did people react?
• Bought land and built farms and homes in Kirtland • Opened a store, temple, mill and printing press • Became prosperous • Outnumbered non-Mormons • Set up a bank that failed during the national banking crisis of 1837.	• Became jealous of Mormon success • Were afraid they would be outnumbered by Mormons • Became angry when they lost their savings • Drove the Mormons out of Kirtland.

Missouri 1837–38

What did the Mormons do?	How did people react?
• Bought land and built farms and communities mainly in Caldwell County • Became prosperous • Were friendly with Plains Indians • Wanted to free slaves • Set up a secret police force, the **Danites**.	• Mistrusted Mormon attitudes to slaves and Plains Indians • Became frightened of Danites • Attacked Mormons and burned down their houses • State governor sent in troops to restore order • Threw Joseph Smith into prison • Drove Mormons out of Missouri.

Illinois 1838–46

What did the Mormons do?	How did people react?
• Re-built decaying town of Commerce • Re-named Commerce 'Nauvoo' and made it a prosperous community • Practised **polygamy** • Criticised Joseph Smith for being a 'dictator' • Chose Brigham Young as their leader.	• Governor of Illinois granted Nauvoo a charter • Became afraid they would be out-numbered by Mormons • Mobs assaulted and killed Mormons • Smith imprisoned and killed by a mob • Governor cancelled Nauvoo's charter • Governor told Mormons to leave Illinois • Brigham Young organised emigration.

For discussion

What were the most important 'push' factors that drove the Mormons to move west?

What evidence is there in the above chart that the Mormons would be able to cope with the difficulties of settling in the West?

Brigham Young: trail organiser

Brigham Young's first jobs as leader were to organise the move of 1,500 men, women and children into dangerous, unknown territory and to help them survive a journey they had not expected to have to make and for which they were poorly prepared.

They were travelling 2,250 km to the Great Salt Lake and land that no one else wanted. Young:

• divided the Mormons into manageable groups, each with a leader
• insisted on strict discipline, giving everyone a specific role to play
• taught them how to form their wagons into a circle at night for safety
• insisted on regular resting places.

The advance party followed the ruts made by the wagon wheels of the ill-fated Donner party. Would they suffer the same fate? Reaching the top of the pass that led down to the Great Salt Lake in July 1847, the group had to decide whether to press on to the fertile lands of Oregon and California, or descend to the infertile, empty salt flats that surrounded the Great Salt Lake. Brigham Young is supposed to have said, 'It is enough. This is the right place.' His sister-in-law, Harriet, arriving a few days later, felt differently – see Source B.

The main party, fleeing from Illinois, arrived at the Great Salt Lake in August 1847. But as the months and years passed, Mormons arrived almost continuously as wagon train after wagon train got through to the valley of the Great Salt Lake.

Source B: From the diary of Harriet Young, Brigham Young's sister-in-law.

> My feelings were such as I could not describe. Everything looked gloomy and I felt heartsick. Weak and weary as I am, I would rather go a thousand miles further than remain in such a desolate and forsaken spot as this.

Source C: A description of the Salt Lake valley, written by one of the first settlers.

> A broad and barren plain hemmed in by mountains, blistering in the burning rays of the midsummer sun. No waving fields, no swaying forests, no green meadows. But on all sides a seemingly endless waste of sagebrush – the paradise of the lizard, the cricket and the rattlesnake.

Source D: The Byington family, all Mormons, photographed in 1867, resting on their way to the Great Salt Lake. They are, left to right at the back: Elizabeth (6), Nancy (37), Nancy (17) and Hannah (30). Left to right in the front: Hyrum (8), Jannette (2) and Joseph Henry (39). The elder Nancy and Hannah were Joseph Henry's wives.

Brigham Young: planner and organiser

The Great Salt Lake, and the land surrounding it, was hardly ideal for founding a settlement. The lake itself, as you will have guessed, was salty, and the lands surrounding it too poor to grow crops on. Brigham Young's sister-in-law was not the only person to feel dismay.

1 Establishing Salt Lake City

The first months were hard. Many died from cold and hunger, and grasshoppers devoured the summer's crops. So how did Brigham Young turn this hostile and unpromising land into a flourishing state? He had one huge advantage: he had total control over his community, which obeyed him without question and believed that God inspired all his decisions. One of the first decisions he made formed the basis for future success. He decided that no one owned any land, water or timber: it would all be fairly allocated by the Mormon church. This had a tremendous impact on the design, efficiency and prosperity of the settlement at Salt Lake.

Water was a problem as the water in the Salt Lake was useless. However, the streams supplying the lake were sweet (i.e. not salty) and the Mormons together dug a main irrigation ditch from them through the farmland; side ditches were dug so that all the land could be irrigated, and people were given exact times when they could draw water from the main irrigation ditch.

2 Spreading throughout Utah

Brigham Young's plan was that Mormons should spread throughout Utah. He had every part of the territory surveyed in order to find out where it would be possible to farm. Once an area was found to be suitable, a town was marked out and irrigation ditches dug, and settlers were chosen to make sure that there was a balance of skills, ages and occupations. In order to make the boundaries of Brigham Young's territory secure, some towns, such as Las Vegas, were planned along its boundary.

Source E: How land was allocated in Salt Lake City and the surrounding area.

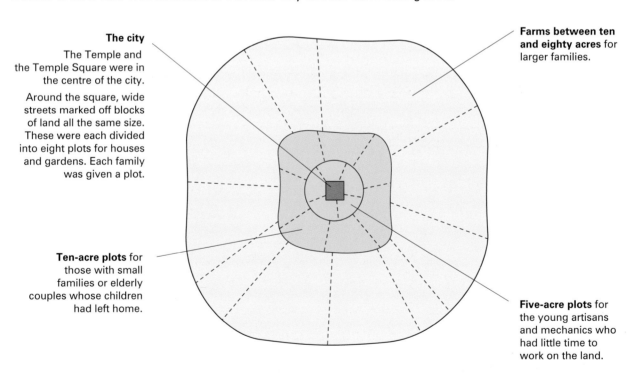

The city
The Temple and the Temple Square were in the centre of the city.

Around the square, wide streets marked off blocks of land all the same size. These were each divided into eight plots for houses and gardens. Each family was given a plot.

Farms between ten and eighty acres for larger families.

Ten-acre plots for those with small families or elderly couples whose children had left home.

Five-acre plots for the young artisans and mechanics who had little time to work on the land.

3 Encouraging emigration

If the Mormon territory of Utah was to flourish, it needed thousands and thousands of settlers to work in the cities and on the land to create prosperity. Brigham Young set up a Perpetual Emigration Fund to provide money for poor Mormons living elsewhere in America and in Europe to make the journey, bringing with them the range of skills needed. The response was tremendous. In England alone, 32,894 converts were ready to leave by the end of 1851. They were given a complete financial package to help them travel from their home towns to Utah. They had to repay this money once they were in Utah.

Brigham Young: politician

Brigham Young wanted the Mormons to be free to follow their own beliefs and customs, free from outside interference. In order to do this, they had to be politically independent. In 1847, the Salt Lake valley was part of Mexico, not the USA. When the war between the USA and Mexico ended in 1848, large amounts of Mexican territory, including the valley of the Great Salt Lake, became US territory.

Steps to independence

4 The US government agreed to let the Mormons live their own lives in their own way without interference.
BUT
Utah could not become a state until the Mormons agreed to ban polygamy. In return, the Mormons agreed to a non-Mormon governor and in 1890 they banned polygamy.

3 1857: the US government sent a non-Mormon governor to Utah along with 1,500 soldiers to enforce federal rule.
BUT
A massacre of migrants led to the Mormons blaming the Indians and the non-Mormons blaming the Danites. Tension was mounting when suddenly the US government changed its mind and decided to try to reach a peaceful settlement with the Mormons.

2 The US government appointed Brigham Young to be the first governor of the new state of Utah.
BUT
Although laws were made in Washington and not by the Mormons, Brigham Young began using the Danites to crush opposition from non-Mormons.

1 1848: Brigham Young applied to the US government for the Mormon lands around the Great Salt Lake to become a state called 'Deseret'.
BUT
The US government allowed Mormon lands only to have territory status, meaning it had to be run by federal officials. The territory had to be called Utah after the Ute Indians who lived there. It was not as large as the Mormons wanted and had no port.

Activities

1 Why did the Mormons find it impossible to live in the eastern states? Copy and fill in the following table.

	Example
Their beliefs	
Prejudice against them	
Their success	
Attitudes to non-Mormons	
Attitudes to Indians and slavery	
Polygamy	

2 Look back at Source D on page 27. Use all the information in this section to describe what experiences the Byington family might have had when they reached the Salt Lake valley.

3 Make a list of the ways in which Brigham Young made sure that the Mormons in the Salt Lake valley were going to prosper. Which one do you think was the most important? Why?

4 How successful was Brigham Young in gaining political independence for the Mormons?

ResultsPlus
Build better answers

Explain why Mormons were able to make a success of settling in the West in the years 1846–90. (12 marks)

You may use the following information in your answer and any information of your own:
- The Mormons had to leave Nauvoo in the spring of 1846.
- The Perpetual Emigration Fund was set up in 1851.
- In 1890, Utah agreed to ban polygamy.

■ **Basic, Level 1 (1–4 marks)**
Answer makes a statement lacking in detail, such as 'Brigham Young was a good leader.'

● **Good, Level 2 (5–8 marks)**
Answer gives information (about the journey West for example), but without linking this to the Mormons' success in settling in Utah.

▲ **Excellent, Level 3 (9–12 marks)**
Answer focuses on the question and considers a range of factors, including leadership, determination, team-work and the role of the US government.

Source F: A contemporary engraving of Salt Lake City in 1873, 26 years after the Mormons arrived.

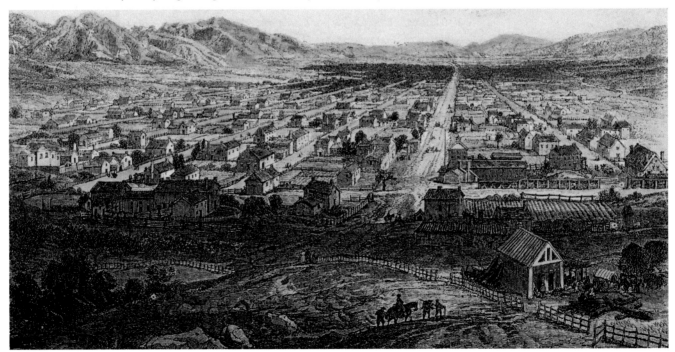

Challenge

The people who crossed the Great Plains in search of a better life, and those who helped them to do so, needed grit, determination, courage and possibly a pinch of desperation. They also needed a large measure of common sense, some basic skills and the ability to solve problems. Use the information in this section, and your own research, to complete this grid that compares some significant individuals.

	Jim Bridger	George Donner	Joseph Smith	Brigham Young
Personality				
Strengths				
Weaknesses				
Problems faced				
Achievements				
Failures				

Is there any one quality you would regard as essential?

For discussion

Does the picture of Salt Lake City (Source F) prove that Brigham Young was a good leader?

Summary

- The trappers and mountain men began the process of opening up the West. They were the first white men to see the fertile lands that lay beyond the Rockies and Sierra Nevada, and news of their discoveries gradually spread east across America. When the market for furs in the East and in Europe collapsed, they became guides to the wagon trains travelling west.

- The banking collapse in the East and subsequent farming crisis in the Midwest led to many contemplating a move to the Far West. The first wagon train to cross the Great Plains arrived in Oregon in 1843 and in California the following year. Soon tried-and-trusted wagon trails were established, but expeditions could still go disastrously wrong as the experience of the Donner party shows.

- The discovery of gold in California led to the gold rush of 1848, involving not only Americans but also people from around the world. Subsequent discoveries in 1858–59 in the Rockies and beyond led to a west-to-east migration of miners. The growth and development of mining towns created problems of law and order and in particular the use of vigilante groups. Nevertheless, the discovery of gold led ultimately to the economic development of the West and the pre-eminence of California as a finance centre.

- The Mormons were forced, because of persecution, to establish themselves on the land around the Great Salt Lake that no other group of migrants wanted. The genius of Brigham Young created a prosperous city from a barren land. From 1847 onwards, Mormons flocked to the area and worked hard, making it prosperous. Clashes with the US government ended when the Mormons agreed to accept a non-Mormon governor of their territory – Utah, which finally became a state in 1890 when the Mormons agreed to abandon polygamy.

1.3 Farming on the Plains

Learning outcomes

By the end of this topic you should be able to describe, explain and understand:

- the importance of the concept of **manifest destiny** in encouraging settlement on the Great Plains
- the role of the government and in particular the importance of the Homestead Act of 1862
- the contribution made by women to settlement on the Plains
- the problems faced by the homesteaders and the extent to which they found solutions.

Getting an overview

Steps to settling the Plains

1874 Major living and working problems solved by many homesteaders

1873 Timber and Culture Act allows homesteaders to claim more land if they can plant trees on half of it

1862 Homestead Act allows settlers to register claims legally on public domain land in the open Plains

1861–65 Civil War leaves ex-soldiers and freed slaves looking for land

1860–90 Railroad building takes settlers on to the Plains

1860s US government makes grants of land to railroad companies

1860s Most land in Oregon and California has been bought up

Activities

You read in the last section about the early settlers who crossed the Great Plains to make what they hoped would be a better life for themselves in the Far West. The Plains were just one of the barriers they had to cross. What would make people stop and decide to settle there?

1 Look back to pages 20–28 and list the problems anyone thinking about settling on the Plains would have to face. Which do you think were the most serious?

2 Now look at 'Steps to settling the Plains'. Which do you think were the most important in helping to solve the problems you identified?

3 Look again at 'Steps to settling the Plains', and at the involvement of the US government. Why would the government, at this time, want to become involved in settling people on the Great Plains? Think of as many reasons as you can.

This section focuses on the **homesteaders**, on the problems they faced in settling on the Plains and on the extent to which solutions were found. As you work through this section, think about:

- the reasons why the US government wanted to see the Great Plains settled
- the impact such settlement had on the US economy
- the impact such settlement had on the native Indians.

Manifest destiny: a neat solution to a practical problem?

In the introduction to this book you read how, by 1853, force, treaties and money had enabled the USA to win the whole of the continent of America from the Atlantic to the Pacific coast and from the Canadian to the Mexican borders. Turn back to the map on page 2. You should be able to work out what worried the US government about the acquisition of this land:

- Would Mexico become strong enough to challenge the American hold on Texas and California?
- Would France regret the sale of Louisiana?
- Would Great Britain try to alter the Canadian border?

One solution was to fill these lands with men and women who were loyal to the young USA.

These men and women would, it was argued, build homesteads and towns, railways and roads, and would farm, mine and trade. They would help make the USA strong, prosperous and able to defy any enemies. This was, of course, only one solution to the problem, but it was a solution that quickly became part of a dream. This dream had begun to grow in the minds of Americans even before they gained their independence from Great Britain – the dream that the whole of America would be settled by white Americans. Gradually, they came to believe that this was the right and natural thing to do. Not only was it right and natural, but it was something that clearly had to happen. It was their manifest destiny.

How was the 'manifest destiny' dream developed?

John O'Sullivan, editor of the New York newspaper *The Morning Post*, was the first person, as far as we know, to use the term 'manifest destiny'.

Source A: From *The Morning Post* 1845.

> It is our manifest destiny to overspread and to possess the whole of the continent which providence has given us for the development of the great experiment of liberty.

In 1860 the American Congress asked the artist Emanuel Leutze to paint a picture that put the concept of 'manifest destiny' into visual form.

Source B: Emanuel Leutze called this picture *Westward the course of Empire takes its way*. It is painted on a wall inside the Capitol building in Washington, DC.

Source C: This engraving, made in 1868 by Frances Flora Bond Palmer, is also called *Westward the course of Empire takes its way*. It has appeared in more US school books than any other picture.

How was the USA to be governed?

You have already read about what happens when law and order do not keep up with settlement. Look back to page 24 to remind yourself. These territories, newly settled, would need firm and clear government. The system of government, decided on in 1787 in Philadelphia by representatives from the original 13 states, was planned so that it could be extended to lands beyond the Appalachian Mountains. It was a system of government that allowed the states their independence yet at the same time enabled them to work together as one country. What they came up with was a **federal** republic. The federal government made decisions for the whole country, such as whether or not to go to war. Individual states made decisions such as whether or not to have the death penalty or retain slavery. This system of government has continued until the present day.

Activities

1   Look at Sources B (on page 33) and C. How far do they give the same impression of the American dream of manifest destiny?

2   Study Source D on page 35. What are (a) the strengths and (b) the weaknesses of this system of government? Where does real power lie?

For discussion

What do you think were the problems involved in implementing the American dream of manifest destiny?

Source D: How the US was governed in the 19th century.

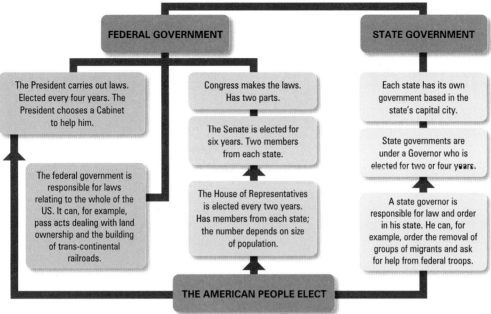

The following text appears within the diagram:

FEDERAL GOVERNMENT

STATE GOVERNMENT

The President carries out laws. Elected every four years. The President chooses a Cabinet to help him.

Congress makes the laws. Has two parts.

Each state has its own government based in the state's capital city.

The federal government is responsible for laws relating to the whole of the US. It can, for example, pass acts dealing with land ownership and the building of trans-continental railroads.

The Senate is elected for six years. Two members from each state.

State governments are under a Governor who is elected for two or four years.

The House of Representatives is elected every two years. Has members from each state; the number depends on size of population.

A state governor is responsible for law and order in his state. He can, for example, order the removal of groups of migrants and ask for help from federal troops.

THE AMERICAN PEOPLE ELECT

How did the US government help people settle on the plains?

It was clear that the US government wanted Americans to settle on the Great Plains. There were several ways in which government action helped this to happen.

Public domain land

All land opened for settlement in the West was called 'public domain'. This meant that it belonged to no one and could, therefore, be settled by anyone or left empty. The US government decided to change this by trying to make sure that all land had an owner. The land was surveyed and divided into parcels of 9.6 km^2 called townships. Each township was divided into sections of 640 acres each and offered for sale at $1 per acre. This was far too expensive for ordinary settlers, and the **speculators** moved in, buying up the land and selling it on at a high price to those people who could afford to pay. This was not what the government intended.

The Homestead Act 1862

Desperate to stop land speculation and settle ordinary families on the Plains, the government passed the Homestead Act. This Act enabled settlers to claim a quarter-section of land to live on and farm. This claim had to be entered in an official land register. After five years the settler could pay just $30 and get a certificate of ownership. In other words, the land for settlement was virtually free. It was at this point that the settlers began to be called 'homesteaders'.

The Timber and Culture Act 1873

The government realised that 160 acres was not enough to support a homesteader family. This Act allowed a homesteader to claim a further 160 acres if he promised to plant trees on half of it.

The Desert Land Act 1877

This gave settlers the right to buy 640 acres of land cheaply in areas where lack of rainfall was a more-than-usual problem.

The railroads

In order to encourage the newly formed railroad companies (see pages 48–51) to expand across the Plains, the government gave them township land parcels on either side of the tracks they were laying. Obviously this was not the only incentive the railroad companies had, but it certainly encouraged both railroad building and settlement.

In 1869 the Union Pacific Railroad Company and the Central Pacific Railroad Company completed the first railroad across the Great Plains. By 1893 there were six companies that connected the Mississippi–Missouri rivers with the Pacific coast. Between them they owned about 155 million acres of land on the Plains. In order to make the railroads pay, the companies had to sell this land. Money from the sale of the land was used to finance more railroad building. Furthermore, the sale of the land would, the companies hoped, attract more passengers and freight as more people would travel west and live and work there.

Source A: The railroad companies began a massive advertising campaign in America and Europe. This poster was produced in 1875.

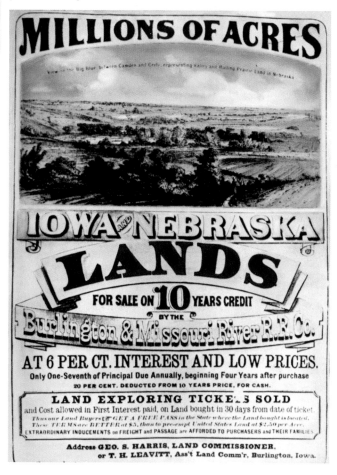

How did the homesteaders build homes for themselves?

Once a claim was staked and registered, all families faced the same problem: how to build a house that was solid, safe and secure and that would withstand the extremes of weather experienced on the Plains. They had to build with the raw materials that they had on their own land, and for most families this came down to the bare earth beneath their feet. First by hand, and later with specially built ploughs, they cut blocks of earth (sods) to use as building bricks. Because of this, the homesteaders were nicknamed **sod-busters**.

Sod houses were solid and strong. They had to withstand gales and storms, drought and blistering heat, grasshoppers and prairie fires. They also had to house men, women and children, and keep them warm enough and well enough so that they could work hard to make a living from the prairies outside.

It took about an acre (0.4 hectares) of land to provide enough sods to build an average-sized sod house on the Great Plains. The walls were about a metre thick, and the house was roofed with grass and more sods. Once a house was built, it would be plastered with wet, clay-like mud, which set hard and made the house more or less watertight.

Sod houses may have seemed warm and cosy, but in reality they had many drawbacks.

What work did women do on the Great Plains?

It was an achievement to build a house out of sods for yourself and your family. It was even more of an achievement to live in a sod house successfully and to manage day-to-day living so that your family was kept warm, fed, clothed, clean and healthy. This, inevitably, was the work of the women. The contribution made by women to the successful settlement of the Plains did not go unrecognised by officialdom: in 1869, women in Wyoming Territory were given the vote, nearly 50 years before women in Britain.

How did homesteaders settle on the Great Plains?

The first people to decide to try to settle on the Plains faced enormous problems: how to live on the Plains and how to farm them. They solved these problems in different ways and with different degrees of success. Some stayed and became prosperous farmers; others quit altogether. In between came the thousands who struggled on, always convincing themselves that tomorrow would be better.

Source A: The sod house of the Cram family in Loup County, Nebraska, 1886.

Source B: From C.G. Barns *The Sod House,* published in 1970.

Contagious diseases were common. The common drinking cup, the open well, the outdoor toilet (or no toilet at all) shared the blame with the lack of ventilation and crowded quarters of the sod house. The floor was commonly of clay dirt. It was not possible to scrub or disinfect it of the millions of germs that found a breeding place in the dirt trodden underfoot. Spitting was common. No wonder the death rate from diphtheria was so great among children. While the houses were, as a rule, warm in winter and cool in summer for the human occupants, they favoured fleas and bed bugs by the million. Added to the lowering of vitality by lack of a balanced ration of food, lack of clothing, and changes of temperature, the wonder is not so much that disease and infection took a heavy toll. The wonder is that so many survived.

Fuel and food

Every homesteader needed fuel. Without fuel the homesteader family would be cold, hungry and dirty. There were hardly any trees on the Plains, and so no wood to burn. The sod-buster's wife therefore collected barrow loads of dried cow and buffalo dung, of which there was plenty.

This burned well, but quickly. Charley O'Kieffe remembers watching his mother bake biscuits (see Source C).

Source C: From C. O'Kieffe *Western Story: The Recollections of C. O'Kieffe*, published in 1960.

Stoke the stove, get out the flour sack, stoke the stove, wash your hands, mix the dough, stoke the stove, wash your hands, cut out the biscuits with the top of the baking powder can, stoke the stove, wash your hands, put the pan of biscuits in the oven, keep on stoking the stove until the biscuits are done.

Activities

1 What were (a) the advantages and (b) the disadvantages of sod houses?

2 Both Indians and homesteaders lived on the Great Plains. In order to do so, they had to solve the problems of building a home there. The Indian solution was the tipi; the homesteaders' solution was the sod house. Explain how and why these solutions were so different.

Source D: From M. Sandford *Journal of Mollie D. Sandford 1857–66*, published in 1959.

> For breakfast we had corn bread, salt pork and black coffee. For dinner, greens, wild ones at that, boiled pork and cold corn bread washed down with 'beverage'. This turned out to be vinegar and brown sugar and warm creek water.

Meals were often monotonous and very boring, as Mollie Sandford, a schoolteacher living with a homesteader family, found out (see Source D).

Dirt, disease and babies

People and clothes had to be kept clean and so did houses. Spiders, fleas and all kinds of insects lived in the earth walls and floors of sod houses. Even with modern detergents and vacuum cleaners it would have been impossible to keep such a house really clean. The homesteader woman had an uncertain water supply, little soap, some rags, and brushes made from twigs. She fought an unending battle against dirt and disease. All the women had well-tried remedies for illness, which they adapted to life on the Great Plains. For example, they would put warm manure on a snake bite, pour urine into an ear that was aching, wrap a cobweb around a cut and persuade someone with measles to eat a well-roasted mouse. When women got pregnant and gave birth on the Great Plains there were no gynaecologists, maternity hospitals or community midwives to help them. They simply got on with it.

A woman's work is never done!

Women homesteaders had to improvise with the materials they had available on the Plains in order to try to maintain their family's living standards.

Teachers and teaching

Not all the women who travelled to the Great Plains were married. In 1845, the recruitment of women teachers for sod schools on the Plains began. As late as 1859, a Kansas paper, the *Lynne County Herald*, printed an advertisement for 'One hundred schoolmarms, who will pledge themselves not to get married within three years'. Schoolteachers were needed to teach the children living on the Great Plains and in the growing townships. The pay was usually low, and most lived with the families of the children they taught. The

Source E: Extracts from the 1839–42 diary of Keturah Penton Belknap, who was a homesteader in Iowa.

> All this winter I have been spinning flax and tow to make summer clothes. I have not spent an idle moment and now the wool must be taken from the sheep's back, washed and picked, and sent to the carding machine and made into rolls, then spun, coloured and woven for next winter. I can't weave so I spin for my mother-in-law and she does my weaving.
>
> … Now it is harvest time. I am tending the chickens and pigs and because we have two cows I make a little butter.
>
> … I have got my work for the winter pretty well in hand. Have made me a new flannel dress coloured blue and red. I am going to try to make me one dress every year, then I can have one for best and with a clean check apron I would be all right. I made some jeans enough for two pairs of pants for George.

Source F: Thomas Allen Banning wrote about his mother's work in his autobiography.

> I have often wondered how my mother stood it with such a family of children and no one to help her except my oldest sister. We used candles, which my mother made by pouring melted tallow into moulds. We used soft soap that my mother made by leaching water slowly through a barrel of wood ash to get the alkali and potash, and then boiling this in a kettle with the scraps of fat she saved. Often she would sit up late at night darning our socks and mending our ragged trousers.

'schoolmarm' did not have to struggle in the same way as the homesteader's wife, but she had to struggle against prejudice and ignorance, and she had to work in appalling conditions (see Source G). Nevertheless, the 'schoolmarms', by insisting on certain standards of behaviour and speech, did a great deal to make the West a more civilised place.

Creating a community

Women looked after their husbands and children and created a home for them. But it was a very isolated life. Homesteads were often several kilometres apart and families could become very isolated. With the men out farming, it was often left to the women to make the connections between

Source G: R. Holt wrote 'The Pioneer Teacher', which was published in 1955. Here he describes the experiences of one schoolteacher on the Plains.

> When she asked each child to bring his own drinking cup, a delegation of school directors appeared demanding to know the reason for such nonsense. She won the argument and proceeded to other matters. There was not the slightest sign of a toilet. When she told the directors that she could not teach if they did not build one, one of them remarked 'Now you see what comes of bringing someone from Outside. Never had any trouble before. Plenty of trees to get behind.'

the homesteads. The support of another family was essential in times of trouble, and it was good to celebrate with others when the harvest was better than expected or a new baby was born. The children, too, needed more than their brothers and sisters to play with and get to know. So how was a sense of community developed? This was the work of the women. The men may have met other farmers and discussed problems such as the Indians, ranchers and buffalo. But it was the women who worked together to develop a sense of community.

Source H: From C.G. Barns *The Sod House*, published in 1970. Barns was a doctor on the Great Plains in 1878.

> Our neighbourhood people were a fine class of people. Social gatherings were common as were the lunches of fried chicken, cake and delicacies. The sod schoolhouse had given way to a small frame building. This became the public hall for all entertainments, social gatherings, Sunday School and religious services.

Farming on the Great Plains: the problems

Most of the people who set up as homesteaders on the Plains had had experience of farming in the East of America or in Europe. However, the soil and climate on the Great Plains were different from anything they had experienced before. No one had ever farmed the Great Plains. No one knew which crops to grow nor how best to prepare the land. All the homesteaders could do, initially, was to use the methods that they knew worked elsewhere.

Activities

1 Make a list of the work done by the women homesteaders.

2 Create a spider diagram to show how these jobs enabled families to live on the Plains.

3 How did the women help settlements develop on the Plains?

For discussion

What was the most important work done by the women homesteaders?

Ploughing and sowing

Before crops could be grown, homesteaders had to plough the ground so that seed could be planted. The Great Plains had never before been ploughed. The grasses that grew there had roots that formed a dense, tangled mass at least 10 cm deep. The cast-iron ploughs that many homesteaders brought with them bent and buckled under the strain and had to be repaired constantly. Making the land productive was a slow and back-breaking job.

Water

An average of 38 cm of rain fell on the Great Plains in a normal year. This was simply not enough to sustain agriculture. To make matters worse, it fell at the wrong time: in the summer, when the sun and hot winds dried up what little moisture the soil had retained. Crops would not grow well and sometimes did not grow at all. In the second half of the 19th century, for example, a series of severe droughts hit Kansas and Nebraska. No rain fell between January 1859 and November 1860. A regular supply of water was clearly essential.

The 'old' solutions would have been to irrigate or dig a well. On the Great Plains, irrigation was impossible because there were no lakes or rivers from which to dig drainage ditches. Many farmers did dig wells, but this was an expensive and uncertain business. In any case, homesteaders with wells of their own rarely had enough water to irrigate their crops properly. Everyone went short as the precious water was shared among those who needed it.

Land holdings

The size of a homesteader's holding was clearly important. It had to be large enough to support himself and his family, and small enough for him to work himself or with family help. The government allocation (see page 35) of 160 acres could not yield enough to support the average homesteader and his family.

Crops

At first, the homesteaders planted the crops they knew best. They planted maize and soft winter and spring wheats. These crops did not do well on the Plains, with their low rainfall, scorching-hot summers and extremely cold winters. In order to make farming a profitable business, farmers have to grow crops that will fetch a good price. It was the same for the homesteader, except that he first had to find a crop that he could grow successfully.

Fencing

Homesteaders needed to fence their land so as to make a clear boundary between their claim and the claims of their neighbours, and to stop cattle straying onto their claim and destroying the crops they were trying to grow. However, they did not have any timber with which to build fences, and hedging plants would not grow quickly enough, even if they survived.

Devastation: fire and grasshoppers

Homesteaders had to cope with many hazards, but the most terrifying of these was fire. In the summer and autumn, when the prairie grasslands were bone dry, the merest spark could set off a fire that ran wild. Homesteaders could beat out small fires. However, once fire took hold, all the homesteaders could do was hide inside their sod houses while their crops were destroyed, their animals burnt to death and the fire burnt itself out.

Source A: Homesteaders trying to make a living on their land in Nebraska in the 1880s.

Devastation came, too, from another source that was every bit as deadly. Between 1874 and 1877, Rocky Mountain locusts (grasshoppers) swarmed through the prairies, devouring everything in their way. It seemed there was nothing they would not eat: crops and tree bark, leather boots and buckets, wooden door frames – even washing.

Most homesteaders were determined to survive on the Great Plains. However, if they were to do more than simply survive, they needed to find new ways of farming. New inventions, discoveries or techniques were needed if the homesteaders were to succeed and prosper.

Activities

1 The homesteaders faced many problems as they struggled to make a living by farming the Great Plains.

   (a) Make a list of the problems.

   (b) Which problem (or problems) were short term and had to be solved immediately?

   (c) Which problem (or problems) were long term and had to be solved if they were to stay on the Great Plains for years and make a success of farming there?

   Copy and complete the grid below.

Problem	Short term or long term?
Crops did not grow well.	

Farming on the Great Plains: the solutions

The women adapted very quickly to living in a sod house. The men took longer to change their old ways of farming. This was partly because it took a long time for them to realise that the old methods simply were not suitable. It takes many months to realise that a crop is not growing properly, and several years to realise that one bad year is not an accident but that all years will be bad.

Machinery

Gradually the factories in the East of the United States began to mass-produce farm machinery. Mechanical reapers, binders and threshers became cheaper. Ploughs were built with steel ploughshares that cut through the soil easily. Furthermore, mass-produced machinery came with spare parts and so could easily be repaired out on the Great Plains if something went wrong. From the mid-1880s farm machinery helped the homesteader cultivate more land without needing more men. A man with a sickle and flail could harvest only 7.5 acres (3 hectares) of wheat in the same time that a man with a mechanical reaper could harvest 100 acres (40.5 hectares). It was the railroads (see pages 42 and 48–53) that made this possible.

Wind pumps

Farmers could not always hold on to the land they staked out on the dry and arid plains. Many gave up because they could not find water – or because they could not find *enough* water. There was always water below the surface soil, but sometimes it was a very long way below. The homesteaders needed some mechanical means of raising water to the surface that was cheap to build and run, and that could produce water in a steady flow.

Cattlemen and railroad builders used wind pumps, and these were quickly adapted to meet the needs of the farmer. First, a high-powered drill was used to get down to the water, which was sometimes several hundred metres below the surface. Then a wind pump was built to raise the water to the surface. It was hardly surprising that, from the mid-1880s, a towering wind pump dominated most of the homesteads on the Great Plains.

41

Source A: A wind pump on a homestead in Custer County, Nebraska, in 1888.

New techniques and crops

Dry farming was a technique learned by the homesteaders. Farmers ploughed their land whenever it rained or snowed. This created a fine film of dust, which settled on top of the soil, trapping the moisture beneath and preventing it from evaporating. In this way, homesteaders conserved water and grew better crops.

The soft wheats, which the early homesteaders planted, did not do well. This was largely because of the very hard winters and the hot, dry summers of the Great Plains. In 1874 a group of Russian migrants arrived on the Great Plains. They brought with them 'Turkey Red', a variety of wheat that grew well in the harsh Russian climate. By 1881 the homesteaders had worked out a way of grinding this new, hard wheat. Growing 'Turkey Red' wheat, using the dry farming method, was beginning to be very profitable indeed.

By itself, none of these inventions, discoveries and developments would have ensured success for the homesteader. Some were more important than others. Some were more important than others at different times and in different places and for different people. What is vital is that they all came together at the right time to enable the homesteaders, by 1890, to control the Great Plains. The homesteaders were no longer forced to change their lives to adapt to the Great Plains. They were able to force the Great Plains to become rich, fertile farmlands beyond the wildest imaginings of the early pioneers who crossed the Plains to get to Oregon and California.

Barbed wire

In 1874, Joseph Glidden invented barbed wire. Barbed wire meant that the homesteaders could fence their land quickly, efficiently and cheaply. They could plant crops knowing that herds of cattle would not stray on to their land, and trample and eat growing crops. They could experiment with animal breeding, knowing that stray bulls would not mate with their stock. However, in using barbed wire to protect their own livelihood, the homesteaders destroyed that of other people.

Railroads

Railroads made it possible for the homesteaders to prosper on the Plains by bringing machinery, goods and materials to them and by enabling their produce to be sold in more and more distant markets. You can read more about this on pages 48–53.

Legislation

The US government finally realised that 160 acres of land was not enough for successful farming on the Great Plains. The 1873 Timber and Culture Act (see page 35) meant that the ordinary homesteader, who could not afford to buy more land, could make a reasonable living.

> ### For discussion
>
> Look back at the photograph of the Nebraska homesteaders in Source A on page 40. What advice would you give them?

Activities

1 Create a table listing the problems involved in farming on the Great Plains and matching them with solutions. Remember, not all problems had solutions, and some problems had more than one solution.

2 Would it be true to say that, by 1895, the homesteaders' problems had been solved? Use the information in this chapter in your answer.

3 Indians and homesteaders lived on the Great Plains but their lifestyles were very different. Where do you think the points of conflict between them would come, and why?

Challenge

Were all homesteaders successful on the Great Plains?

Homesteaders reacted in different ways to the problems they faced. Read Source B below.

Use the information in this chapter to explain what the reasons might have been for these homesteaders giving up.

Source B: Part of a report in a Kansas newspaper, *The Gazette,* in 1895.

> There came through yesterday two old-fashioned wagons headed east, four horses, very poor and very tired, and one sad-eyed dog. A few farm implements of the simpler sort were loaded in the wagon. For ten years they had been fighting the elements. They have tossed through hot nights, wild with worry, and have arisen only to find their worst nightmares grazing in reality on the brown stubble in front of their sun-warped doors. They had such high hopes when they went out.

 Results**Plus**
Build better answers

Describe the part new technology played in solving the problems of farming. (9 marks)

 Basic, Level 1 (1–3 marks)
Answer gives examples of new technology, such as 'machinery was brought by railways'.

 Good, Level 2 (4–6 marks)
Answer gives detailed information about the use of new technology by farmers.

 Excellent, Level 3 (7–9 marks)
Answer explains the way in which new technology could be used to solve specific problems. For example, how and why the use of wind pumps solved the problems of drought and improved crop yields.

Summary

- The concept of 'manifest destiny' was one that envisaged the whole of America being populated by white Americans. The American people came to believe that this was the right and natural thing to do. Indeed, it was their manifest destiny so to do. The government encouraged this, as it wanted keep all the land it held between the Pacific and Atlantic oceans and one way of doing this was to fill it with white Americans who were loyal to the US government.

- The US government helped people settle on the Great Plains by passing the Homesteader Act in 1862, which enabled a homesteader to claim 160 acres cheaply, and the 1873 Timber and Culture Act, which allowed a further claim of 160 acres if the homesteader promised to plant half of it with trees.

- Homesteaders settled on the Great Plains, building sod houses from the materials they found there. The work done by homesteader women in keeping their families fit and well was essential if farming there was to be successful.

- The early homesteaders faced enormous problems in farming the Plains involving the lack of water, the extremes of climate, the search for appropriate crops and the need for new techniques. These had largely been solved by 1895.

Inhabitants and early settlers

Quick quiz

1 Are the following statements true or false? If they are false, what is the correct answer?

	True or false	Correct answer
Plains Indians believed that people were more important than all other living creatures.		
Plains Indians held dances for fun.		
Plains Indians depended on the buffalo for their survival.		
Mountain men were hunters and trappers.		
Jim Bridger was an important gold miner.		
Gold was discovered in California in 1858.		
Mining settlements were lawless places.		
The Mormons were expelled from Kirtland, Missouri and Illinois.		
Joseph Smith masterminded the success of Salt Lake City.		
Brigham Young wanted to call the Mormon state 'Deseret'.		
George Donner took his wagon train into California.		
Manifest destiny meant that it was the destiny of the Indians to control the Great Plains.		

Revision activity

2 The following paragraph is not an accurate account about the homesteaders:

- Find the mistakes.
- Replace them with the correct words or phrases.

> In 1862 the US government passed the Homestead Act in order to prevent people from settling on the Great Plains. The homesteaders built their homes from timber. The Timber and Culture Act of 1877 forced the homesteaders to replace the trees they had chopped down. Wind pumps helped the homesteaders divert water from streams and rivers on to their own land. 'Turkey Red' was a new breed of turkey that did well on the Plains. Barbed wire meant that the homesteaders could fence off their land quickly and cheaply.

Checklist

How well do you know and understand:

- ● the Plains Indians' beliefs
- ● the Indians' way of life on the Great Plains
- ● the ways in which, and the reasons why, Plains Indians fought
- ● the reasons why different groups of migrants moved west
- ● the importance of the concept of 'manifest destiny'
- ● the reasons for the long-term success of the Mormons in Salt Lake City
- ● the impact of the gold rush and the mining towns on the Great Plains
- ● the role of the government in encouraging settlement on the Great Plains
- ● the contribution made by women to the settlement of the Great Plains
- ● the problems faced by homesteaders and the extent to which they found solutions?

Help required!

3 Your local primary school is putting on an exhibition for children aged 7–11 to show them how Indians lived on the Plains. They have asked for your advice. You must decide what to include in the exhibition and also think of a snappy title. Remember:

- the age of the children when selecting suitable material
- that there is only one display panel with room for about six items
- the need for accuracy and balance.

ResultsPlus
Watch out!

Students often confuse the command words 'describe' and 'why was'. Remember:

Describe means give details of features.

Why was means that you should give reasons and explain.

Student tip

Quite often students confuse the migrants who crossed the Great Plains to settle in Oregon and California with the migrants who settled on the Plains and became the homesteaders. The peak year for migration across the Plains was 1850. People did not begin settling on the Plains in any great numbers until after the passing of the Homestead Act in 1862.

Development of the Plains

Introduction

At the start of the great push westwards, the Plains were seen as an obstacle to be crossed. But once the early pioneers had established themselves in Oregon and California, they needed to keep in contact with the eastern states. They needed to buy and import supplies, they needed a market for their produce and they needed to keep in touch with family and friends. As townships grew and developed on the western seaboard and in mining areas, law enforcement officers, US government officials and administrators needed fast, reliable access to the western territories. There was also tremendous pressure from the US army, who had built forts and garrisons throughout the West to protect settlers and traders, and who needed to keep them garrisoned and supplied.

The key to meeting all these needs and demands was the railroad. The construction of railroads opened up the Plains and was one of the factors that enabled the cattle industry to develop, first by encouraging the long drives of cattle to the **railheads**, and then by enabling ranching and the growth of cow towns. However, these developments on the Plains were far from easy. The Great Plains were not empty prairies. They were inhabited by roaming tribes of Indians who followed the great herds of buffalo and by homesteaders who, in ever-increasing numbers, were staking claims to the land and beginning to farm it. Conflict of increasing severity seemed inevitable.

Aims and outcomes

By the end of this section, you should be able to describe, explain and understand:

- the importance of the railroads in the development of the West; the role of government, the problems of construction and the impact of the railroads on homesteaders, cattle ranchers and Plains Indians

- the reasons for the growth of the cattle industry after 1865; the reasons for the move onto the Plains, the development of cow towns, and the causes of the subsequent boom and bust of the industry

- the changing role of the cowboy: cattle drives, changes in the nature of ranching from open range to fenced pasture; the contribution of Charles Goodnight, Joseph McCoy and John Iliff

- the problems of lawlessness in the early settlements and the role of government and local communities in tackling this; the roles of sheriffs, marshals, judges and vigilantes including the roles of Wyatt Earp and Jesse James and the significance of Dodge City; the reasons for conflict between homesteaders and cattle ranchers leading to the Johnson County War.

FASCINATING FACT

Of the cowboys employed on trail drives between 1866 and 1885 12 per cent were Mexican and 25 per cent were black.

Buffalo Bill and the chief of the Cave-Dwellers struggled on the edge of the precipice, locked in deadly embrace, while the brave Navajo, tomahawk in hand, kept the other Indians at bay.

cattle drover a cowboy who herded cattle along the trails

chuck wagon a wagon where cowboys kept food and cooking utensils while travelling the trails

corral an enclosure for cattle or horses

lynching hanging without trial

marshal a man appointed by the US President to be responsible for law and order in a state or territory

pony express a rider on a fast pony who carried mail across the Plains before the railroads

posse van a coach full of armed guards attached to a train

railhead a station where cattle were picked up for transporting to the eastern states

riding shotgun armed men riding on a stagecoach to protect it from attack

rustling stealing animals that were part of a herd

sheriff a lawman appointed, usually for two-year periods, to be responsible for law and order in a county

teetotaller a person who does not drink alcohol

watershed a ridge or high piece of land from which water flows in two different directions

Activities

1 What impression of the West is given by the 'dime' novel cover above?

2 Is the impression a correct one? Work in pairs and look back over the work you have done so far to work out whether a situation such as this could have happened.

3 Why do you think cheap novels such as this one were so popular? (Think back to the work you did on manifest destiny.)

2.1 The construction of the railroads

Learning outcomes

By the end of this topic you should be able to describe, explain and understand:

- the aims and role of the government in promoting railroad construction
- the aims and role of the railroad companies in planning and building railroads
- the problems of railroad construction
- the impact of railroads on farmers, cattle ranchers and Plains Indians.

Activities

People do not hold fancy ceremonies for no reason. Look carefully at Source A and then answer the following questions:

1 What different sorts of people can you see in the photograph?

2 How can you tell that the railroad companies thought the meeting of the two railroads was an important event?

3 What do you think was the significance of this event for the development of the West?

4 How were the railroads helping to fulfil the American concept of 'manifest destiny'?

Source A: A photograph of the Golden Spike ceremony at Promontory Point, Utah, on 10 May 1869. This was where the Union Pacific Railroad that started in Nebraska met the Central Pacific Railroad that started in California.

As you work through this section, think about three things:

- What were the motives of the railroad builders and promoters?
- What impact did the railroads have on those living and working on the Great Plains?
- How did the railroads help the US economy develop?

Railroads from coast to coast

Before the 1860s, all railroads stopped at the Mississippi and Missouri rivers. Only 30 years later, a network of railroads spanned North America. How had this happened? Why were stagecoaches, the **pony express** and the telegraph not good enough to link the east and west coasts?

Why did the US government support railroad development?

As early as 1853, the US government paid $150,000 to have possible transcontinental railroad routes surveyed. However, the existing railroad companies had neither the confidence nor the money to risk building tracks westward. By the 1860s, the situation had changed. By 1860, the US government was keen to get involved in railroad development for a number of reasons:

- Railroads would enable the government to bring law and order to the territories in the West, and in doing so would help create a sense of national unity.
- Trade links with countries in the Far East (such as China and Japan) could be made from ports in Oregon and California. Railroads were essential to get goods for export to these ports.
- Railroads would be another way to help fulfil manifest destiny by making it easier for would-be migrants to reach uninhabited areas of America.

These motives were put into practical effect in 1862, when Congress passed the Pacific Railways Act. This set up two companies: the Union Pacific Railroad Company and the Central Pacific Railroad Company. Union Pacific began laying track going westward across the Plains from Omaha, Nebraska, beside the Missouri River. Central Pacific began in Sacramento and went east.

Why did the railroad companies risk building railroads across the Plains?

The railroad companies took the risk because, when it came to it, the risk was small. Railroad companies, like any other company, existed to make a profit for their shareholders. These were people who had bought shares in the company and were paid money, called a dividend, from that company's profits. If, in any one year, a company did not make a profit, then the shareholders did not get a dividend. So branching out into a new venture meant that both the company and the shareholders were taking a risk. In order to minimise this risk, the railroad companies accepted the US government's offer of free land. They could therefore build tracks without having to spend shareholders' money on land. The land on each side of the tracks could either be used as security for bank loans, or could be sold to would-be settlers and the money raised could be ploughed back into the company. It looked like a win-win situation.

What problems were involved in railroad construction?

The most basic problem was, of course, funding the railroad projects, but you have seen how this was managed. Even then, building a transcontinental railroad was far from easy:

- *Land.* Railroads had to cross the most difficult terrain in the USA: mountains, valleys and deserts. These stretched the skills of the engineers and construction workers to the limit.
- *Living and working conditions.* Railroad labourers lived and worked in squalid conditions. They faced driving rain, hail, gales and snow. They depended on food transported hundreds of kilometres in less than ideal conditions and without refrigeration. They died in their hundreds.
- *Labour shortages.* This was a continual problem. In 1863, the Central Pacific Railway Company solved this difficulty by using immigrant Chinese labour. Between 7,000 and 10,000 additional workers were brought in from China. When the US government set a final deadline for completion of the railway (10 May 1863), Irish labourers were brought in and the deadline was met.

- *Indians*. These remained a problem for white men, just as white men were a problem for the Indians. Indians harassed the railroad builders, desperately afraid that their hunting grounds were being taken away from them.

Even so, the railroad workers built fast and built well. They built about 11 km of track each day on the Great Plains, and they built the Dale Creek Bridge, which was 38 m high and 150 m long, in one month. At that time and under those conditions, it was an amazing achievement.

Source A: Chinese workers building a section of railway through the Sierra Nevada in 1867.

What impact did the early railroads have on the USA?

In 1850, there were about 20,000 km of railroads in the USA. By 1890, there was over 324,000 km of track. Most of this new track was built in the West. Six huge transcontinental lines straddled the country from east to west, and there were hundreds of branch lines reaching out to small, isolated communities.

What benefits did the railroads bring?

The benefits brought by the railroads affected many different groups of people. As you read through these benefits, think about who would have benefited directly and who would have benefited indirectly.

- The actual building of the railroads created a lot of jobs. Work such as surveying and tracklaying, digging cuttings, and building viaducts and tunnels needed different sorts of skills from a large and mobile workforce.
- The demands of railway building – for iron, steel and timber, for example – led to tremendous growth in the industries that supplied the railroad building programme.

Source A: Routes taken by transcontinental railroads by 1895.

- Government officials and law enforcement officers could travel relatively easily from coast to coast, bringing all American people under the same federal laws.

- Wind pumps and drills, barbed wire and mechanical reapers, threshers and binders, steam traction engines and ploughs, essential to the prosperity of the farmer on the Great Plains, were not manufactured on the Plains but were brought to the homesteaders by the railroads.

- The railroads brought furniture and fabrics, dresses and trousers, boots and shoes, stoves, pots and pans and oil lamps into homes on the Great Plains.

- Agricultural produce was sold in more and more distant markets, creating a demand that increasingly prosperous farming could meet.

- The opening up of new markets meant that cattle ranching on the Plains could grow and a thriving cattle industry could develop.

- Cities, for example Denver, Dallas and Los Angeles, grew and flourished in the West.

- Commercial companies began trading with China and Japan, using the growing west coast ports.

- Contact with relatives living far away was made easier, strengthening family bonds.

- The railroad network provided the opportunity for thousands of new settlers to travel to the West.

The US railroad-building boom coincided with the USA's industrial revolution, which it helped to create. Indeed, by 1890 the USA was the world's leading industrial power, with a rail network that was bigger than that of Europe, including Great Britain and Russia.

What about the Plains Indians?

The railroads had a devastating effect on the Plains Indians. Indians attacked the railroad builders because they suspected that the railroads they were building would affect their way of life. They were right. But the railroads did not just affect the Indians' way of life: they played a large part in destroying it:

- Indians' freedom to roam the Great Plains, hunting the huge herds of buffalo, was severely hampered by the railroads that criss-crossed the Plains.
- The railroads that brought goods and materials to homesteaders and ranchers enabled their enterprises to grow and develop.

- The homesteaders and ranchers fenced in their farmlands and ranches. This meant that the days of the open prairie were gone and the Indians could no longer roam over them, following the buffalo.
- The Indians' attitude to those who had, in their eyes, invaded and taken over their homelands, changed to one of almost total hostility. The Plains, which they believed no one could own, had been taken over, violated by people with different lifestyles and different values.
- The Plains Indians relied almost wholly on the buffalo to support and maintain their way of life. (Look back to page 9 to remind yourself why this was.) Buffalo hunting became a sport among the white men, with special excursion trains taking the hunters onto the Plains.

Source B: A contemporary engraving showing hunters shooting buffalo from a train 'for sport'.

Activities

3 The section 'What about the Plains Indians?' gives five factors that brought about change to the Plains Indians' way of life. Put them in order of importance and explain why you have put the factors in this order.

4 Think back over this section. The railroads brought great benefits for some and destroyed the lives of others. On balance, would you agree that the advantages they brought outweighed the disadvantages?

ResultsPlus
Build better answers

Why were the railroads so important in the development of the Great Plains? (16 marks)

You may use the following in your answer and any other information of your own.
- The first transcontinental railroad opened in 1869.
- Abilene was built on the Kansas-Pacific railroad.
- Mechanical reapers were carried by rail to the Plains from factories in the East.

 Basic, Level 1 (1–4 marks)
Answers offer a limited amount of information, for example 'cattle were driven to railheads'.

 Good, Level 2 (5–8 marks)
Answers describe the uses of the railways in some detail.

 Better, Level 3 (9–12 marks)
Answers explain, with detailed information, some of the ways the railways were important, for example showing their role in changing the cattle industry or making farming more efficient.

Excellent, Level 4 (13–16 marks)
Answers explain why the railroads were important, showing, with detailed information, their impact on all aspects of life and the development of the Plains, including: law and order, farming, ranching, the way of life of the Plains Indians.

For discussion

Suggest ways in which the Plains Indians could have stopped their way of life being destroyed.

Challenge

To what extent did the railroads help fulfil the American dream of 'manifest destiny'?

Summary

- The US government supported railroad development because it wanted to encourage trade to the Far East, boost the US economy, bring law and order to the West and achieve manifest destiny. It demonstrated support for railroad development by passing an Act that set up the Union Pacific and Central Pacific railroad companies, and by making grants of land to the railroad companies on which they could build tracks and attract settlement.

- Railroad companies took the risk of investing in railroad development because government support made it likely that shareholders would get a good return for their money.

- Problems of railroad construction involved difficult terrain, hostile Indians, an unreliable workforce and the need for financial support. Even so, 11 km of track were laid every day, and on 10 May 1869 the Union Pacific and Central Pacific railroads met at Promontory Point. A transcontinental railroad had been built.

- Railroads impacted on homesteaders and cattle ranchers by supplying goods and materials that they needed, and by enabling them to reach more and more distant markets. Railroads impacted on Plains Indians by enabling the destruction of their way of life.

- Railroads stimulated the American economy by consuming manufactured goods themselves and by delivering manufactured goods throughout the USA.

- Railroads enabled law and order to be established in far-flung communities, bringing all American people under one federal law. By linking distant communities, railroads enabled families to stay in contact with each other, thus creating a cohesive community.

2.2 Cattlemen and cowboys: the rise and fall of the cattle industry

Learning outcomes

By the end of this topic you should be able to describe, explain and understand:

- the reasons for the growth and the collapse of the cattle industry after 1865
- the contribution made to the cattle industry by Charles Goodnight, Joseph McCoy and John Iliff
- the changes in ranching
- the changing role of the cowboy.

Getting an overview

In this chapter you will learn about the boom and bust of the cattle industry, about long drives and ranching. One of the common threads that runs through everything you will find out about is the cowboy. Look carefully at this annotated drawing and use it to answer the question in the activity section.

Activity

1 What conclusions can you draw about a cowboy's life and work from this drawing? Copy the grid below and enter in your conclusions.

Item	Conclusion
Bandana	
Saddle	
Heeled boots	
'Chaps'	
Lariat	
Stetson	

As you work through this section, keep checking to see if you were right!

The hat (stetson) was made of felt. The broad brim protected the wearer from the sun and was an umbrella in rainy weather. In winter it could be pulled down over the ears and tied – giving protection from frostbite.

The saddle was the cowboy's throne – its bumps and contours grew to fit the owner's body. A man might gamble away his money, horse or chaps, but he would put his saddle on his back and return home on foot.

The bandana was the handkerchief (usually red) which was worn around the neck, and for use as a mask. When the cowboy rode along behind the herd of cattle, he pulled the handkerchief up over his nose and mouth to protect him from the dust.

A lariat or lasso.

The 'chaps' were an overgarment like a pair of trousers with a cut-out seat. Many were made of the shaggy skin of a bear, goat or sheep. They were also made to withstand the thorny vegetation and the cutting north wind, and to protect the legs from chafing during a long ride and in the case of a fall.

All cowboys wore high-heeled boots. The heel and arch were so constructed that the foot and leg were comfortable when riding. Spurs were worn at all times.

The cattle industry: from trails to boom

You have seen how the early settlers regarded the Great Plains as an obstacle to be crossed – and then the homesteaders found ways of living and farming on them. It was the same with cattlemen and cowboys. First they drove the cattle across the Great Plains, and then they found ways of raising the animals on them.

Beginnings in Texas

After the war between the USA and Mexico ended (see the map on page 2), white American Texans took over the herds of longhorn cattle left behind by the retreating Mexicans. As the demand for meat grew, unofficial trails were established as the Texan cowboys drove the longhorns to markets in New Orleans, California and Chicago, and Texan cattle ranchers became rich. However, the Civil War (1861–65) put an end to all this as Texans left to fight on the Confederate, and losing, side. When those who survived returned, they found huge herds of cattle running wild. With few people to look after them, the longhorns had toughened up in order to survive and had bred until there were about 5 million of them roaming the grasslands of Texas.

Establishing the trails

The returning cattlemen knew that the growing cities in the North would pay about $40 per head of cattle, ten times the price beef fetched in Texas. They rounded up the cattle, hired cowboys and began to organise regular drives to the northern cities. It was here that the new railroads helped. By driving cattle 800 km or so to the new railroad, the cattlemen could get their cattle easily to the growing towns in the Midwest and in the East. In 1866, for example, about 260,000 head of cattle from Texas crossed the Red River, making for Sedalia, the railhead on the Kansas Pacific Railroad. There the cattle were loaded into wagons and taken east to St Louis and then north to Chicago.

A special case: the Goodnight-Loving Trail

When Charles Goodnight returned home to Texas after the Civil War he, too, found that his herd was running wild and had increased enormously in size to about 8,000 head of cattle. However, instead of driving a couple of thousand cows to the nearest railhead to reach markets in the East, he did something entirely different. He had heard that US troops were holding 7,000 Navaho Indians captive on a reservation near Fort Sumner in New Mexico, and that the Indians were close to starvation. Here was a marketing opportunity! Charles Goodnight teamed up with Oliver Loving, an experienced **cattle drover**. They hired 18 cowboys, selected 2,000 cattle from Goodnight's herd and set up a **chuck wagon** that would hold all the supplies they would need on this new drive. The lack of water nearly ruined

Source A: Cattle trails and cow towns in the south-west USA.

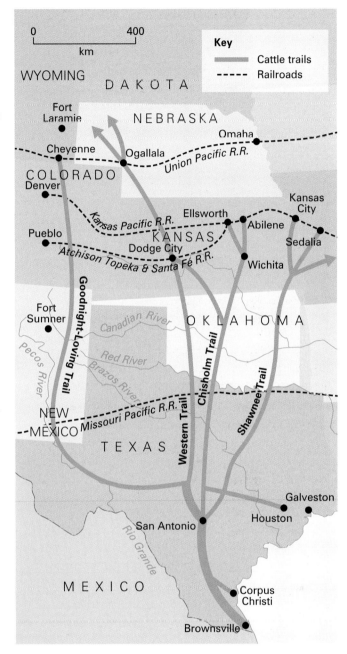

the expedition. Cows, horses and men all suffered, and many animals died before they reached the Pecos River, rest and lush grass. Even so, when they reached Fort Sumner, Goodnight and Loving still had 1,700 head of cattle to sell. These fed the Indians on their reservation and the army in its fort. So began Goodnight's profitable career in the cattle industry, supplying the US army and Indian reservations as far north as Fort Laramie.

Problems with the cattle trails

There were problems with all the cattle trails:

- In south-east Kansas, south Missouri and north Arkansas, armed mobs attacked cattlemen on the cattle trails. They were afraid that a deadly tick, carried by the longhorns but not affecting them, would infect cattle on the land through which the trails passed.
- Rustlers on all the trails were prepared to fight and kill to get the longhorns for themselves.
- Hostile Indians were a problem on every trail. Indeed, Oliver Loving died in 1867 as a result of wounds inflicted by a Comanche raiding party.
- The Goodnight-Loving Trail avoided hostile white mobs in Missouri and Kansas and, to a certain extent, hostile Indians, but it suffered from a lack of water and was too far west for the eastern markets. It was the eastern markets that were bigger and more profitable, and therefore the ones that most cattlemen wanted to reach.

Cattlemen were desperate to get their cows to the markets in the eastern states. Some tried to establish trails further and further east, driving their cattle to railheads at Sedalia and St Louis. But the grass along these new trails was poor and the animals arrived for shipment in poor condition. How could the cattlemen use the best trails and avoid all the problems?

Joseph McCoy and Abilene – the solution to a problem?

Joseph McCoy found the ideal solution to the problems of the long trails. Instead of having the cattlemen drive their herds to the railheads and load them on to a train to be taken to markets in the East where they would be sold, his plan was to set up cow towns in the West. It would be in these cow towns that the southern cattleman and the northern buyer would meet on equal footing to buy and sell the herds. They would be undisturbed by rustlers, aggressive mobs and hostile Indians.

And so it was Joseph McCoy who built the first cow town – Abilene – on the Kansas Pacific Railroad. It was to prove enormously popular.

Although initially Abilene was nothing more than a collection of huts, it had all the grass and water needed when thousands of cattle gathered there, waiting to be sold. McCoy had timber brought in and built offices, cattle pens and a small hotel. In 1867, cattlemen took about 37,000 cattle along the Chisholm Trail from San Antonio to Abilene. By 1870, the number of cattle passing through Abilene had grown to over 300,000, and Abilene had three more hotels and ten saloons. Between 1867 and 1881, nearly 1.5 million head of cattle passed through the town. McCoy had been right about the need for a cow town. More were to follow the success of Abilene. So began the beef bonanza.

Boom!

As the railroads moved westwards, new cow towns (Dodge City and Newton, for example) developed. New trails were blazed to connect with the railroads at these points. They were enormously successful. In the peak years of the beef bonanza, 1867–85, nearly 4 million cattle passed through the cow towns. A quarter of a million head of cattle passed through Dodge City alone, to be taken by railroad to such places as Chicago and Kansas City. There were huge profits to be made. A cow worth $5 in Texas could be sold for ten times that amount in the cow towns, and Joseph McCoy and other cattle dealers took a commission on every head of cattle sold through their towns. It was a win-win situation: everyone prospered, from saloon owners to cattle dealers, from cowboys to timber merchants.

Activities

1. Describe the ways in which the Goodnight-Loving Trail was different from the other trails.
2. What was a cow town? Why did the cattlemen and cowboys not simply keep on driving their cattle to the railheads?
3. How important were the railroads to the prosperity of the cattle industry?

The cattle industry: from ranching to bust

The cattle trails and cow towns were, as you have seen, enormously successful. However, the last great drives north were in 1886. By 1895, the drives were over. What had changed?

Why did the cattle drives end?

- The railroads across the Great Plains made many cattlemen rich. But they also brought people who began to settle on the Plains (see Section 1.2) and the homesteaders' farms began to block the trails.
- In 1868, the US government and the chiefs of the northern tribes agreed the Fort Laramie Treaty (see page 76). Now the Indians began to make the cowboys pay to drive the cattle across Indian land.
- The cattlemen began to believe it would be easier to raise cattle on the Plains instead of driving cattle across them.

John Iliff: a successful entrepreneur

John Iliff was an entrepreneur with an eye for the main chance. As a young man he had set up as a trader in Kansas, selling food and goods to travellers on the Oregon and Californian trails; when gold was discovered, he moved further out to supply the miners with the goods they needed. So it was no surprise when he decided to try his hand at being a cattleman, but a cattleman with a difference. He began to graze cattle on the Plains. This was the beginning of ranching. Iliff's business grew and prospered.

- He enlarged his herd by buying Oliver Loving's cows, which were being driven to Colorado.
- He experimented with breeding and produced cows that had sweeter meat than the Texan longhorns. They were less hardy, but this did not matter as they did not need to survive the long drives.
- He won a contract to supply meat to the Union Pacific Railroad construction gangs.
- He sent his beef to cities in the eastern states using the newly invented refrigerated railroad cars that meant the animals could be slaughtered before being transported.

- He won a contract in 1872 to supply beef to Red Cloud and over 7,000 Sioux Indians who had been moved by the US government to land near Fort Laramie.

Others watched what John Iliff was doing and copied him. Ranching on the Great Plains had begun in earnest.

What was the 'open range'?

The ranches on the Great Plains were 'open ranges', unfenced land that was claimed, but not owned, by the ranchers. Every rancher had 'range rights' over the land he claimed. This included the right to reserve a stream or waterhole for his cattle, and often the boundaries between ranches were **watersheds**. At the centre of the ranch were the buildings where the ranch-hands lived and worked: bunkhouses and living quarters for the cowboys; stables for the horses; and barns for storing fodder, harnesses, bridles and saddles. As the land was unfenced, the cattle roamed freely, grazing where the grass was best. Because of this, each cow was branded on its shoulder or hindquarter to show to which ranch it belonged. Branding also tended to prevent **rustling**, where thieves could steal and drive off cattle that did not belong to them.

The years 1880–85 were the peak years for ranching on the Plains. Ranching was seen as a sure-fire way of making money.

But there was trouble ahead.

Source A: Figures for the cattle industry on the northern Plains taken from the tenth census of the USA, 1880.

State/territory	Number of cattle in 1860	Number of cattle in 1880
Kansas	93,455	1,533,133
Nebraska	37,197	1,113,247
Colorado	None	791,492
Wyoming	None	521,213
Montana	None	428,279
Dakota	None	140,815

Bust!

- *Overstocking.* As cattle prices rose, ranchers put more and more cows on the open range. This put pressure on the grass, and the drought of 1883 made the problem worse because the grass withered. Overstocking, even in good times, was not a clever idea. The situation was worsened when the price of cattle fell (see below) and more ranchers kept their cattle instead of taking them to market.

- *Demand.* In the eastern states, beef was so readily available that shops had to lower their prices in order to sell the meat they had bought. This meant that the prices paid for cattle carcasses fell. There was simply too much meat about. Cattle fetched lower and lower prices at the Chicago stockyards. By 1882, profits from cattle ranching were beginning to fall. Some ranchers sold up and the price of cattle fell even further. Others kept their cattle on the ranches, waiting for better times.

- *Climate.* The cold, blustery winter of 1885 hit cattle and ranchers hard. The summer that followed was so hot that grass withered and streams dried up. The following winter was the worst in living memory. Temperatures fell as low as –55° Celsius. Cattle could not reach the grass through the deep snow and they died in their thousands. At least 15 per cent of the herd perished, along with cowboys. Many cattlemen went bankrupt.

The boom days were over.

A new way of ranching

It now seemed sensible to create smaller units producing high-quality meat. Animals could not be allowed to wander freely because breeding had to be carefully managed. Ranchers began fencing in their land, using the newly invented barbed wire, which enabled large areas of land to be fenced quickly. At first this brought them into conflict with the homesteaders, who claimed the ranchers were cutting them off from their water supplies. A second invention solved this problem. Wind pumps meant that ranchers could find water almost anywhere on their ranches, and portable wind pumps gave the ranchers even greater flexibility – they could take the pump to the herd rather than the other way round. The days of the open range were over, but technology enabled a new way of ranching to develop.

- This was much less dependent on the weather. Smaller herds could easily be found when the snows closed in and brought closer to the ranch buildings where there was shelter and food. In times of drought, water could easily be found.

- It was also much more sustainable. Smaller units were much more manageable than the large open ranges and made better use of the resources found on the ranches.

The investment needed to make the new ranches successful happened only because the open range system came under pressure. These problems made possible a whole new, and successful, approach to cattle raising on the Plains.

What was the life of a cowboy like?

Sources A and B were both painted by men who had had experience of life in the West and who knew a lot about cowboys. Both paintings give more or less accurate images of the life of a cowboy, but at different times in his work cycle. Cowboys were mostly young men – black Americans and Indians, Spaniards and Mexicans, as well as white Americans. Many were former

Activities

1 Draw a spider diagram showing the reasons why the open range came to an end.

2 Who, in your view, contributed most to the development of the cattle industry: Charles Goodnight, Joseph McCoy or John Iliff?

For discussion

Could the boom and bust of the cattle industry have been avoided?

Confederate soldiers, desperate for work; a lot were drifters and some were criminals on the run. Hard-living, hard-drinking men, they were rarely married and took full advantage of the brothels and saloons in the cow towns when work was done.

Trails and drives: organisation

The cowboys rounded up the cattle in the spring and sorted out which were to go on the long drives. The cowboys might drive their own boss's herd, or several herds, and the trail of cows could be as long as 2 km. Organisation was essential. Each had a specific job so that the animals did not wander off and the drive was kept up to speed.

For discussion

Why do you think artists, film-makers and novel writers were so fascinated by the lives of cowboys?

Source A: *In without knocking* by Charles Russell was painted in 1909. Russell worked on ranches in the years 1880–92.

ResultsPlus
Build better answers

Give two things you can learn from Source A about the life of a cowboy. (4 marks)

■ **Basic, Level 1 (1–2 marks)**
Answer makes an inference but does not use the source to support it. For example, 'it suggests cowboys let off steam after work because they are shown crashing into the saloon and firing pistols in the air'.

● **Good, Level 2 (3–4 marks)**
Answer uses the source to support the inference. For example, 'the source suggests that cowboys were hard-living men who rode into town to the saloons and hotels at the end of a period of hard work'. 'The horses are ridden hard suggesting the men desperately needed relaxation, but nevertheless look fit and well cared-for, suggesting they were essential to the cowboys' work.'

Source B: *On the trail* by Frederic Remington, who worked on a sheep farm in Kansas and travelled widely in the West.

Activities

1 Describe the ways in which the life of a cowboy changed between 1865 and 1895.

2 Sources A and B are both paintings. Look at them carefully. Choose one of the cowboys. How might he have explained how he ended up doing what he was doing in the painting you have chosen?

Trails and drives: dangers and problems

Cowboys moved the herd fast to start with, and then slowed it down to about 20 km a day. This enabled the cows to graze as much as possible and so be fat for the market when they finally arrived at their destination. But it was not easy. There were dangers and problems at every turn.

- Stampedes were frightening and usually happened during the first days of the drive, when the cows were nervous and ready to bolt at anything: a flash of lightning, the whinny of a horse or a roll of thunder. Once a stampede had started, the cowboys worked frantically to turn the herd in on itself so that the cattle, circling at speed, would exhaust themselves.

- Wildlife was abundant on the Plains. Wolves could be particularly troublesome, as could scorpions and poisonous snakes.

- Water, vital for keeping man and beast alive, was also treacherous. Rivers had to be crossed and undercurrents could be dangerous. Quicksands could drown a horse and rider, or a cow, within minutes.

- Indians were unpredictable, sometimes friendly, sometimes aggressive, and, given the lack of buffalo, always ready to steal some cows.

- Night – when the cows were contained within one or more rope **corrals** – was the time when most cowboys could relax. Even so, cows had to be guarded. Cowboys not on night-watch slept in the open and most had the ability to fall asleep anytime, anywhere.

Ranching

Ranching, and the end of the drives, changed the work patterns and the lives of the cowboys. They still rounded up cattle and branded them, and they still took cattle to market. But they also had to 'ride the line', checking the boundaries of their boss's range to make sure no one's 'range rights' had encroached on those of their boss, looking out for sick animals and animals in distress, and shooting predators. Cowboys' lives were more comfortable. They had bunkhouses in which to sleep, cookhouses where their food was prepared, and somewhere to shelter. It was not always easy to force men used to the freedom of the open range to live on ranches and keep more or less regular hours, and ranch bosses had to make rules. It was common to forbid drinking and gambling, as well as the carrying of guns and knives, while on the ranch.

The establishment of fenced ranches meant that fewer cowboys were needed. For those that remained, their jobs became more mundane and predictable. The wild life of the cowboy was over. It continued only in novels and music halls, films and circuses.

Challenge

Choose a cow town. Use the Internet to research its growth and development. In particular, investigate how it became part of the cattle industry's boom, and what happened to it once the cattle industry declined in the 1890s.

 Results**Plus**
Build better answers

Why did the life and work of the cowboy change in the years 1865–95? Explain your answer. (12 marks)

You may use the following in your answer and any other information of your own:

- In 1866, cattle drives began from Texas.
- By 1880, there were approximately 4.5 million cattle on ranches on the Great Plains.
- During 1865–1886, there were huge losses of cattle owing to drought and a severe winter.

■ **Basic, Level 1 (1-4 marks)**
Answer briefly describes some of the changes, such as 'the long drives ended'.

● **Good, Level 2 (5-8 marks)**
Answer gives information about the life and work of the cowboys, but without linking this to why there were changes.

▲ **Excellent, Level 3 (9-12 marks)**
Answer explains, using detailed information, how the cattle industry changed in the period and why these developments meant that the life and work of the cowboy had to change.

Summary

- The US Civil War interrupted the development of cattle trails from Texas to the markets in the East. After 1865, returning cattlemen established regular trails to railheads at, for example, Sedalia in Missouri, Abilene and Elsworth in Kansas, and Ogallala in Nebraska.

- The Goodnight-Loving Trail was different in that it did not go to a railhead. Charles Goodnight and Oliver Loving supplied the US army and Indian reservations direct, blazing a trail first to Fort Sumner and then to Fort Laramie.

- Problems with the long trails to the railheads (the deadly cow tick, rustling and Indians) led to the establishment of cow towns, where cattlemen and buyers could meet face to face. The first cow town, Abilene, was set up and developed by Joseph McCoy. Others quickly followed. The boom period for the cattle industry began.

- Homesteaders' farms began to block the trails to the cow towns and, under the terms of the Fort Laramie Treaty of 1868, Indians began charging cattlemen for driving cows across their land. A move to ranching on the Plains, spearheaded by John Iliff, began. Iliff was an entrepreneur, supplying meat to railway construction gangs and Indians on reservations, and he used the new refrigerated trucks to deliver carcasses to markets in the East of the USA. Other men followed, and ranching on the Plains began in earnest.

- Overstocking, a fall in demand for beef and the terrible winter of 1885–86 led to the collapse of the cattle industry. The open range came to an end and ranches were fenced.

- A new system of ranching was developed that focused on smaller ranges and controlled breeding for high-quality meat.

- Cowboys' basic responsibilities were the care of the cows, particularly on the long trails. It was a hard life and cowboys tended to be hard-drinking, hard-living men from a range of ethnic origins. With the coming of ranching on the Plains, their work changed – they 'rode the line' spending the winter months doing routine jobs such as fence mending.

2.3 Establishing law and order: problems and solutions

Learning outcomes

By the end of this topic you should be able to describe, explain and understand:

- the reasons for lawlessness in the early settlements
- the role of government and local communities in tackling lawlessness
- the contribution made to the situation by individual lawbreakers and law enforcers such as Jesse James and Wyatt Earp
- conflict between homesteaders and cattle ranchers leading to the Johnson County War.

Source A: This poster is offering a reward for the capture of Jesse James and his gang.

PROCLAMATION
$5,000⁰⁰
REWARD
FOR EACH of SEVEN ROBBERS of THE TRAIN at WINSTON, MO., JULY 15, 1881, and THE MURDER of CONDUCTER WESTFALL
$ 5,000.00
ADDITIONAL for ARREST or CAPTURE
DEAD OR ALIVE
OF JESSE OR FRANK JAMES
THIS NOTICE TAKES the PLACE of ALL PREVIOUS REWARD NOTICES.
CONTACT SHERIFF, DAVIESS COUNTY, MISSOURI IMMEDIATELY
T. T. CRITTENDEN, GOVERNOR
STATE OF MISSOURI
JULY 26, 1881

Activities

1 Read the Source A poster carefully. What does it tell you about law and order in the West?

2 Does this poster make you think that the West was a wild and lawless place or one where the authorities were in control?

Why was the West such a violent and lawless place?

Keeping law and order in the West was a problem in those areas that were growing but where effective government had not been set up. Setting up a system of government took a long time, and meanwhile violent men (and some women) took advantage of the situation and made what they could while they could. Even when a system of government had been set up, it did not always work properly. Men who were supposed to keep law and order were not always honest. Criminals were often able to outwit even honest lawmen.

There were many reasons why the early days for people in the West were so troubled:

1 Travel to and in the West was slow and difficult. Law enforcement men, such as **sheriffs**, could not move around quickly.

2 The new mining towns and cow towns sprang up quickly and the government did not have enough properly trained law enforcement officers.

3 There were many potential causes of conflict between people following different occupations on the same land: cattlemen and homesteaders, cowboys and townspeople; miners and mountain men, for example.

4 There were many potential sources of conflict between different ethnic groups: east-coast Americans, blacks, Chinese, Indians and Europeans, for example, all had different backgrounds, world views, values and ambitions.

5 After the Civil War (1861–65) many ex-soldiers roamed the West, unable to settle to civilian life, bearing grudges and ready to settle old scores.

6 The West was dominated by a rugged individualism: everyone believed they should look after themselves and sort out their own problems. Most people in the West carried guns and so a quarrel was often settled by a shooting.

Activities

3 Give a score out of ten for importance in making the West a lawless place to each of the six reasons given on these pages.

4 Now use that information to create a spider diagram showing how all these reasons were connected.

What crimes were committed in the West?

The many different types of crime that were committed in the West were the same as crimes committed everywhere else in the world: assault, theft and murder. What made the West different was that, in the early days, there were so many opportunities for crime because the rule of law was fairly rough and ready, and because the area attracted many people who, in any case, did not have much respect for the law.

Bank robbery

In the days after the Civil War many of the men who had fought on the Confederate side had no job or army to which to return. Some of them turned to bank robbery. One of the most notorious bank robber gangs was the James Younger gang, led by Jesse James (look back to the poster on page 62), who carried out a series of extremely successful bank raids in the 16 years between 1866 and 1882.

Cattle rustling

The great herds of cattle roaming the Great Plains were easy targets for cattle rustlers. Branding did help prevent rustling (see page 56), but rustlers were usually very good at adapting brands by adding a line here and a circle there. In any case, many cows were rustled when they were calves and before they were branded. Rustlers stole cows to add to their own herds, or in order to start a herd of their own.

Claim jumping

In the early days of gold mining, official law and order (as you read on page 24) was often hundreds of miles away. Late arrivals on the gold fields often tried to steal land from those who had already staked a claim there.

Fence cutting

This was a common crime in the 1880s and 1890s, when homesteaders and small-scale ranchers would cut the barbed-wire fences put up by the large ranches because the fences prevented them getting to waterholes and streams. The large ranches were trying to grab as much land as possible and squeeze the smaller people out.

Horse stealing

Horses were extremely valuable – they were essential if cowboys and ranchers, homesteaders and Indians were to survive on the Great Plains. If horse thieves were caught, they were often hanged. For Plains Indians, horse stealing was an important part of their way of life. It was one of the ways in which Indians gained honour.

Murder

Shootings were extremely common and it is almost impossible to tell how many men were killed in the early days of the West. Some historians reckon the total to be around 600 a year; others argue that the figure is exaggerated. Whatever the truth of the matter, some men became famous gangsters.

Racial attacks

Racial attacks were common in the West. Blacks, Indians and Mexicans were all targets, but the most frequently attacked group was the Chinese. The US government encouraged thousands of Chinese to emigrate to help in the railroad-building programme, which they did most effectively. It seems that most of the attacks on Chinese labourers were by people who were afraid that they were undercutting them in the job market. The worst incident was in 1885 when, in Rock Springs, Iowa, 51 Chinese were killed and more than 400 thrown out of town.

Source A: A still from the cowboy film *Butch Cassidy and the Sundance Kid* (1969) showing the gang carrying out a train robbery.

Trail robbery

Individual travellers, stagecoaches and wagons were all at risk of being held up and robbed as they travelled in the West. Robbers waited until the unsuspecting people were well out of town and then attacked in the vast open spaces where help was hundreds of kilometres away. The US army tried to provide protection from its forts along most of the well-travelled trails. Stagecoach companies employed men to '**ride shotgun**' as guards, but they often were killed in shoot-outs.

Train robbery

Trains, with coaches carrying gold and cash, were easy targets for robbers, and gangs attacked them regularly. Track ran for hundreds of kilometres across open plains far from towns. It was easy to stop a train and rob it without interference from the forces of law and order. The railroad companies responded by strengthening doors and employing armed guards. Later, they built specially reinforced coaches and even attached **posse vans** full of armed guards to their trains.

Gangs and gangsters

There is no doubt that the West was a violent and dangerous place. Butch Cassidy and the Sundance Kid were not invented for the cinema! It is doubtful, however, whether it was all quite as glamorous or as violent as novels and films would lead us to believe.

How violent were the cow towns?

Most of the legendary shoot-outs in the Wild West were set in the cow towns of the Midwest and this was not all fictional. Trigger-happy gangs of high-spirited cowboys, desperate to let off steam after the rigours of the long drive (see page 59) created chaos. Desperate for relaxation and entertainment, they gave the cow towns, particularly Dodge City, appalling reputations for gambling, womanising and gunfights. The reputations, however, were not all deserved, nor deserved for the whole of our period.

Historian R.A. Billington points out that regulations against carrying guns were in force in all cow towns, and that between 1870 and 1885 only 39 men died from gunshot wounds. Only twice were as many as five men killed in a single year – in Ellsworth in 1873 and in Dodge City in 1878.

By 1870, Abilene was large enough to have some form of local government. Officials stopped guns being brought into the town, and in 1872 cowboys themselves were banned.

Activities

1 Sort the crimes usual in the West under the headings of 'Assault', 'Theft' and 'Murder'. Which crimes would pose the biggest problems to law enforcement officers?

2 Put yourself in the shoes of an investigative journalist in the 1880s. Your editor has asked you to write an article on crime in the West. He wants it to be brief and snappy (no more than 150 words) and to grab and hold the attention of the newspaper readers. Do it by the publication deadline!

Famous lawbreakers

There were plenty of petty thieves and small-time gangsters who lived and died violently and whose exploits were largely unrecorded except by those whose lives crossed theirs. There were, however, some gangs and gangsters who were so notorious that their 'fame' reached the east coast of America and beyond.

Belle Starr (1848–1889). Not all gangsters were men. Belle Starr lived with, and sometimes married, a whole string of gangsters as well as a Cherokee Indian called Sam Starr. But she was more than just a gangster's moll. She planned and carried out robberies herself, rustled cattle and stole horses. She was the first woman in the West to be charged with horse theft and served a five-year prison sentence. Her life ended messily: she was shot in the back in 1889, when she was 41 years old.

Billy the Kid (1859–81). Henry McCarty, nicknamed 'Billy the Kid', started his life of crime when he was sixteen. Accused of robbing a Chinese laundry, he fled to Arizona where he became involved in cattle stealing. In 1877, he was arrested for killing Frank Cahill, an army blacksmith, but escaped and worked for John Tunstall, who was murdered. Billy the Kid swore revenge and joined the 'Regulators', a gang led by Dick Brewer. They killed at least five men, including Sheriff William Brady, believing them to have been involved in Tunstall's murder. In 1878, Lewis Wallace became Governor of Mexico and declared an amnesty for everyone involved in the Tunstall dispute. Billy the Kid gave himself up, but was arrested for the murder of Sheriff Brady. Escaping from custody, he formed a gang that specialised in cattle stealing, particularly in Lincoln County where Billy believed a cattleman owed him money. In 1880, Pat Garrett was elected sheriff of Lincoln County and captured Billy the Kid. Billy was found guilty of murdering Sheriff Brady, but escaped from jail by killing his two guards. Undeterred, Garrett hunted him down and killed Billy the Kid in a shoot-out on 14 July 1881.

Jesse James (1847–82). Jesse James, a Confederate supporter, joined the 'Quantrill Raiders' during the American Civil War. The 'Raiders' attacked troops, terrorised communities and murdered individuals they believed to be anti-Confederate. Their worst atrocity came in 1863, when they attacked the town of Lawrence, killing 150 inhabitants and setting fire to over 180 buildings. Once the Civil War was over, Jessie and his brother Frank formed a gang that specialised in robbing banks, trains and stage-coaches. They managed to kill about a dozen people in the process. They operated in their home state of Missouri, as well as Alabama, Arkansas, Iowa, Kansas and Minnesota. Matters went badly wrong for them in 1881 when they tried to rob the First National Bank in Minnesota, and Jesse James killed the bank cashier. Townspeople fought back, killing three of the gang and wounding all the others. Only Jesse and Frank managed to escape. (Look back at the poster on page 62!) Jesse went into hiding, changed his name to J D Howard, and recruited a new gang, which began raiding (and killing if necessary) in Missouri. Thomas Crittenden, the governor of Missouri, offered a reward of $10,000 for the capture of Jesse James. Robert Ford, a member of Jesse's gang, visited Jesse in his home and shot him in the back of his head. Ford was found guilty of murder and sentenced to death. Two hours later, Crittenden pardoned him and gave him the reward.

Activities

3 Draw a timeline starting with 1845 on the left-hand side and ending with 1895 on the right-hand side. On the timeline, plot the lives of Billy the Kid and Jesse James, one above the other.

4 Describe (a) the similarities and (b) the differences between the lives of Billy the Kid and Jesse James.

5 What do the careers of Billy the Kid and Jesse James tell us about law and order in the American West?

How was law and order enforced?

In the 1860s, most of the lands west of the Mississippi River were federal lands. This means that they were not yet states with their own governor and assembly. Look back to page 35 to remind yourself how the USA was governed. The territories were governed directly by the federal government in Washington, DC, which was responsible for, among other things, law and order. It was the responsibility of the federal government to send law officers into the towns and counties of the federal territories, where they usually did their best to establish the rule of law. As territories became states, law officers had to enforce federal law and state law.

Vigilante committees

However, many communities, as you have seen, sprang up in advance of the 'official' law enforcers getting there. This was most common in mining communities where vigilante committees were set up to administer rough justice. Look back to page 24 to remind yourself of the case of Henry Plummer and Bannack, Montana. Once a vigilante committee had identified someone they suspected of committing a crime, they inflicted punishment by **lynching** or running the suspects out of town. There were around 200 vigilante groups operating west of the Mississippi, many of which were run by the leaders of local communities.

How was law-keeping enforced legally?

As well as the hierarchical structure of law officers shown in Source A, there were two more important law enforcement agencies:

- Texas Rangers were set up in 1820 when Texas was still a territory. There were Arizona Rangers, too. Both were small groups of highly efficient and effective lawmen.
- The Pinkerton Detective Agency was a private detective agency. It did a lot of work in the West, bringing criminals to justice. Banks, railroad and stagecoach companies employed Pinkerton detectives to track down robbers and thieves, as well as to provide general advice and protection.

Source A: The structure of law enforcement.

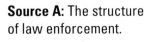

US marshals
Appointed by the President to be responsible for a state or a territory. States and territories were very large so they needed deputies.

Deputy marshals
Assigned to specific towns and counties in the federal territories.

Town marshals
Appointed by townspeople on a yearly basis. Their job was to deal with local outbreaks of lawlessness, like saloon brawls and drunken shootings. They could appoint deputies if necessary. There were fewer town marshals than sheriffs but they did much the same work.

Sheriffs
Appointed in the counties for a two-year period of office. They could force local people to form into a posse to chase local lawbreakers. They could appoint deputies if necessary.

Source B: The states and territories of the USA by 1870.

What happened when suspected criminals were caught?

Suspected criminals were thrown into gaol until they could be tried in a properly convened court of law. Federal judges were appointed by the President – three to each territory – to try cases. The problem was that they had to travel around the territory to which they had been appointed. This meant that accused people often had to wait months for justice. Sometimes local people took matters into their own hands, lynching people they believed to be guilty. The situation usually improved once a territory became a state because the state governor could then appoint judges to try offences against state law.

Who were the law enforcers?

Just as there were legendary criminals, so there were legendary lawmen, who worked hard to uphold the rule of law in circumstances that must have sometimes made their jobs seem impossible.

 William Tilghman (1854–1924). Born in Fort Dodge, Iowa, he spent most of his childhood on a homestead in Atchison, Kansas. Leaving home in 1869, he became an animal hunter and a crack shot; he claimed to have killed 12,000 buffalo. His activities angered local Indians

and, in a skirmish in September 1872, he killed seven Cheyenne braves. Moving to Dodge City in 1875, he opened a saloon (although a lifelong **teetotaller**), and in 1878 he became deputy sheriff and later **marshal** of the city. There he gained a reputation as an honest lawman. Intelligent and crafty, he pursued criminals relentlessly, using disguises and entrapment when necessary, always preferring persuasion to violence, killing only two criminals in shoot-outs. Moving to Oklahoma in 1889, Tilghman established a homestead at Guthrie and worked as a deputy US marshal. Along with Heck Thomas and Chris Madsen (the trio were known as the Three Guardsmen), he was largely responsible for wiping out organised crime in Oklahoma, and was instrumental in rounding up three notorious gangs – the Doolins, the Dalton Gang and the Starr Gang. It is claimed that he was paid more reward money than any other lawman in the West! Retiring in 1910, Tilghman was elected to the State Senate but, missing his old life, he became Chief of Police in Oklahoma City in 1911. He was killed in 1924 while trying to arrest Wiley Lynn, a corrupt probation officer.

Some lawmen crossed and recrossed the line between legal and illegal activities.

Wyatt Earp (1848–1929). Born in Illinois but brought up in California, he was elected constable of Lamar in Missouri in 1870. He was later sacked for horse theft, but he escaped trial and hunted buffalo in Kansas before becoming a lawman in Wichita, where he married the local prostitute. In 1876, he was again sacked from his job, this time for fighting with a fellow officer, but a few months later he was working as deputy marshal in Dodge City, and in 1878 he was appointed assistant city marshal there. Leaving Dodge City a year later, he joined his brothers Virgil, Morgan and James in Tombstone, Arizona. Virgil became city marshal and recruited Wyatt as a 'special deputy policeman'. In 1880, the Earp family quarrelled with two families, the Clantons and the McLaurys, over horse thieving, and Wyatt Earp also started a row with Sheriff John Behan, wanting both his job and his wife. Matters came to a head in October 1881 in a gunfight at the OK Corral, Tombstone. There, according to legend and against impossible odds, Wyatt with his brothers Virgil and Morgan overcame the Clantons and McLaurys. Sheriff Behan promptly arrested Virgil, Morgan and Wyatt Earp for the murder of Tom McLaury, Frank McLaury and Billy Clanton. After a 30-day trial, Judge Wells Spicer, who was related to the Earps, decided that they had been justified in their actions. After this, the Earp brothers struggled to maintain their hold over Tombstone; Virgil was seriously wounded in a bungled assassination attempt, and Morgan was shot and killed while playing billiards with Wyatt. Both suspects for the murder were found dead – supposedly killed by Wyatt. Forced to flee from Tombstone, Wyatt spent the remaining years of his life engaging in petty theft and ended up settling in Los Angeles in 1906. He told his story to Stuart N. Lake, who wrote his biography. This was published in 1931 (two years after his death), but was denounced by Allie Earp, widow of Virgil, as a 'pack of lies'.

Activities

1 Go back to the timeline on which you plotted the careers of Jesse James and Billy the Kid. On the same timeline, plot the lives of William Tilghman and Wyatt Earp, one above the other.

2 What do these timelines tell you about the problems faced by law enforcement officers in the West?

For discussion

Would you describe Wyatt Earp as a lawman or a criminal?

The Johnson County War

Wyoming became a territory in 1868 and a state in 1890. It was well organised and known to be peaceful. Yet, in 1892, in a part of Wyoming known as Johnson County, a fierce and bloody war broke out between two groups of inhabitants: the cattlemen and the homesteaders.

Why did cattlemen and homesteaders clash?

The land in Johnson County was good, and cattlemen and then homesteaders flooded in. But the cattlemen were there first and, besides, were richer and so more influential. They set up the Wyoming Stock Growers Association, to which the state governor belonged, and he used this Association to control the financial policy of the territory and to get laws passed that served the interests of the Association's members.

The mid-1880s were disastrous years for ranchers in Wyoming and all over the Great Plains (see page 58). Homesteaders began taking over land from bankrupt ranchers. Every time they claimed land and fenced it off, especially if it was round a waterhole, the ranchers' anger and resentment grew. Gradually the community became divided into two hostile groups. But the trigger for violence was not fencing the land, but cattle rustling.

Source A: A contemporary engraving showing Ella Watson and Jim Averill being hanged in Wyoming in 1889.

Who was rustling cattle?

The Wyoming Stock Growers Association believed that the owners of small ranches and the homesteaders were rustling cattle from their members, who owned the larger ranches. Soon they had 'proof' of cattle rustling.

Ella Watson and Jim Averill lived together just outside Johnson County and ran a small store, post office and saloon. Ella was a prostitute, and the problem was that some of her clients often paid her with a cow or two that had been rustled. To complicate matters, Ella and Jim rented their land from a rancher, Albert Bothwell, who suspected them of rustling his cattle. Matters came to a head when Jim wrote a letter to a local newspaper, denouncing ranchers as being nothing but rich land-grabbers. This was not the cleverest thing he could have done. Albert had had enough. In July 1889, he and some friends arrived at Ella and Jim's cabin, took them out and hanged them.

Other killings and murder attempts followed, leaving three owners of small ranches dead. Rustling continued. The Wyoming Stock Growers Association hired about 50 gunmen, called the Regulators, to shoot down the troublemakers. In response, the small ranch owners established the rival Northern Wyoming Farmers and Stock Growers Association. The stage was set for a showdown.

From murder to war

By 1892, the Wyoming Stock Growers Association had had enough. It drew up a hit list of 70 people it suspected of cattle rustling and planned a full-scale invasion of Johnson County – with the full knowledge of the governor of Wyoming! The Association hired 22 Texan gunmen to supplement the Regulators, and paid them $5 a day plus expenses with a bonus of $50 for every rustler they killed. They were brought into Wyoming on a train specially supplied by the Union Pacific Railroad Company, and with them came a contingent of newspaper reporters. An invasion of Johnson County was planned. The idea was to capture the town of Buffalo, kill the sheriff and then kill the rest of the men on the Association's list.

Invasion!

The invaders began by cutting the telegraph wires, thus isolating Johnson County from the outside world. In April 1892, under the command of Major Frank Wolcott, the invasion force moved in. Then things began to go wrong. The invaders stopped to attack the KC ranch, where they were held off by Nate Champion and Nick Ray. After Nick was killed, Nate held out all day until he was burned out of his cabin.

Word reached Red Angus, Sheriff of Johnson County, who quickly raised a force of 300 men and went after Wolcott's invaders. Angus's men besieged Walcott's forces at the TA ranch until the US 6th Cavalry arrived and saved them.

Who won?

No one! The defeated cattle ranchers were brought to trial but were never convicted. However, their actions were widely condemned and organisations such as the Wyoming Stock Growers Association were never again able to hold so much power. The homesteaders continued to farm and the ranchers enclosed their ranges. The open range was over.

Activities

1 You now know a lot about homesteaders and ranchers and about the problems involved in keeping law and order in cow towns. Working in small groups, create your own cow town, with gangs and gangsters, a sheriff, cowboys, homesteaders out on the Plains, and ranchers, too. Plan an incident that must be as true to life as possible, using as much information in this chapter as you can. Present this incident to the rest of your class in whatever format you think suitable: a short play, newspaper article, IT presentation, recorded interview – the choice is yours!

2 It is 1895. The US President, Grover Cleveland, wants a report from you on the state of law and order in the West. In not more than 300 words, write that report.

ResultsPlus
Build better answers

Study Source A (see page 62).
Give two things you can learn from Source A about problems of law and order in Missouri. (4 marks)

 Basic, Level 1 (1–2 marks)
Answer takes information from the source or make an inference but does not use the source to support it. For example, 'it was hard to catch criminals, the sheriff relied on people helping him to catch them'.

 Good, Level 2 (3–4 marks)
Answers will use the source to support the inference. For example, 'the source suggests that it was hard to catch criminals like the James brothers. They must have been well known and responsible for several crimes because the notice asks for them by name, and indicates that there have been reward notices out for them before.'

70

For discussion

Who was to blame for the Johnson County War?

Challenge

What part did James Butler 'Wild Bill' Hickok play in the lawlessness of the West?

Activities

What can you learn from the Johnson County War?

3 A study of the Johnson County War will have shown you some of the problems involved in keeping law and order in the West. It will also have given you some ideas about what the solutions were.

Complete the grid below. Remember that not all problems had been solved by 1895, and that some problems had more than one solution.

The Johnson County War: problems and solutions

Problem	Solution
1	
2 Cattle rustling	
3	
4	Arrival of US 6th cavalry
5	
6	

4 What was the most important factor in bringing law and order to the West? Explain your answer.

Summary

- The West was a violent and lawless place. Poor communications made it difficult for law enforcement officers to get to distant communities, and there were too few trained law officers anyway. There were many potential causes of conflict between settlers, and a gun-carrying culture meant that shootings were a common way of settling problems.

- The most common crimes in the West were theft (horse and cattle rustling; bank, trail and train robberies), assault (frequently racial attacks) and murder. Fence-cutting and claim-jumping were frequent in unsettled areas.

- Gangs and gangsters operated in and around cow towns, which gained appalling reputations for violence, drunkenness, prostitution and general lawlessness. Two infamous gangsters were Billy the Kid and Jesse James.

- Law and order was enforced illegally by vigilante committees. These operated before more formal systems were put in place. Once a hierarchy of US marshals, deputy marshals, town marshals and sheriffs was in place, it was easier to control lawlessness. Famous law enforcers include William Tilghman and Wyatt Earp.

- The Johnson County War, where a group of cattle ranchers went with hired guns into Johnson County, Wyoming, to put an end to what they thought was cattle rustling, shows that the West, even by the 1890s, still had places where men thought they could take the law into their own hands.

Development of the Plains

Quick quiz

1 What was it? Match the words or phrases in the box below with their definitions.

Word	Meaning
bandana	cow town
riding the line	unfenced land
vigilante	responsible for law and order in a county
sheriff	a trail
Abilene	unofficial law enforcer
claim-jumping	checking the boundaries of a ranch
open range	responsible for law and order in a territory
rustling	cowboys' scarf
Goodnight-Loving	stealing cattle
US marshal	type of cattle
longhorn	stealing an unregistered claim to land

2 Mind the gap! The paragraph below about the railroads has some missing words. Use the words below to fill the gaps so that the paragraph makes sense and is accurate.

The building of the railroads created a lot of _____, for example _____ and _____. The demands of railroad building led to growth in the _____ that supplied the railroad-building programme. Railroads meant that _____ _____ and _____ _____ _____ could travel easily from coast to coast. Homesteaders prospered because the railroads brought them _____ _____ and _____ _____. Railroads reached markets in the _____ _____ which meant that _____ _____ could develop on the Plains. Cities, for example, _____ and _____ _____, grew in the West. Commercial companies began trading with _____ and _____. Thousands of _____ were brought onto the Plains by the railroads and contact with _____ was made easier, strengthening family bonds.

barbed wire   **cattle ranching**   **China**   **Denver**   **government officials**

industries   **Japan**   **jobs**   **law-enforcement officers**   **Los Angeles**

relatives   **settlers**   **surveying**   **track-laying**   **wind pumps**   **eastern states**

Revision activity

3 Railroads Westward!

A film company is making a short film about the impact of the railroads on the development of the West. The film is to be shown to GCSE students. You are to advise them on what should be included and what should be left out. Remember that you need to consider:

- the railroads' impact on farmers, cattle ranchers and Plains Indians
- the suitability of material you select for a film of this sort
- the need for the material to be short, snappy but accurate.

Storyboard the film sequences and write, or record, a 'voice-over' commentary

Checklist

How well do you know and understand:

- the reasons why the US government supported the railroad companies in promoting and planning railroad construction
- the problems involved in railroad construction
- the impact of the railroads on the West
- the reasons for the 'boom and bust' of the cattle industry
- the contribution made to the cattle industry by Charles Goodnight, Joseph McCoy and John Iliff
- the role of the cowboy and the reasons why it changed
- the reasons why the early settlements were so lawless
- the role of the US government and local communities in tackling lawlessness
- the contribution made by individual lawmakers and lawbreakers such as Jesse James and Wyatt Earp
- the reasons why there was conflict between homesteaders and cattle ranchers that developed into the Johnson County War?

ResultsPlus
Top tip!

When writing about cowboys, trails and ranching, it is very easy to generalise. Don't! Try always to put in a specific fact, name or date when you have made a general statement. The examiners will be impressed.

Student tip

Many students find it difficult to distinguish between 'describe' and 'explain':

- *describe:* give precise details about a key event
- *explain:* give developed causes or consequences of a key event.

Conflict on the Plains

Introduction

A special US government department was set up in 1832 to deal with Indian affairs. It quickly decided that the whole of the Great Plains could be given to the Indian tribes. The Plains were to be one great reservation, to the west of the 95th meridian, which was to be the Permanent Indian Frontier. By 1840, all the Indian tribes to the east of the Permanent Indian Frontier had been moved to the west of it. But that, of course, was not the end of the matter.

The Plains Indians gradually came to be seen as a problem by the US government. They occupied land that was wanted by miners and railroad builders, homesteaders and ranchers. They stood in the way of the United States achieving the dream of 'manifest destiny'. Compromise seemed impossible. Very, very few white people and Indians understood each other. They feared each other, fought each other and betrayed each other as they struggled for control of the Great Plains.

Opinion differed as to the best approach to the problem.

There were the 'negotiators', who believed that a negotiated settlement with the Indians was what was needed. In Washington, DC, many politicians took this humanitarian approach, maintaining that aggressive tactics would only make the Indians more hostile. They believed that the responsibility for Indian affairs should remain with the Bureau for Indian Affairs (later, the Department of the Interior) and should not be handed over to the army.

On the other hand, the 'exterminators', who included most of the homesteaders, ranchers and the soldiers sent to protect them, wanted the Plains Indians exterminated. The Indians, they believed, were lazy savages, posing a problem that was best dealt with by the army. Indeed, the 'exterminators' believed that the Bureau of Indian Affairs should come under army control. It was the tension between these two approaches that led to the Plains Wars being played out as they were.

Aims and outcomes

By the end of this topic, you should be able to describe, explain and understand:

- key events and misunderstandings that led to open conflict, including the Fort Laramie Treaties, Little Crow's War, the Sand Creek Massacre and the completion of the transcontinental railroad
- reasons for, and the impact of, Red Cloud's War and the Great Sioux War, the parts played by Red Cloud and General Custer, and the significance of the Battle of Little Big Horn
- changing attitudes to the Plains Indians after 1876, the government, army and railroads in the destruction of the Plains Indians' way of life, and the significance of the Dawes Act and the Battle of Wounded Knee
- changes to the Plains Indians' culture caused by white settlement, extermination of the buffalo, and life on the Indian reservations.

FASCINATING FACT

General George Custer had long golden curls that came down to his shoulders. He was immensely vain and had lots of photographs taken of himself.

Activities

1 Why was the Permanent Indian Frontier bound not to be permanent?

2 The diagram below shows a pattern of events that happened again and again. Copy it into your file. As you work through this section, add events to each of the five boxes. You could make each box into a spider diagram.

3 What do you think could be done to break a cycle like this? Would the solutions of (a) an Indian and (b) a settler likely to be different?

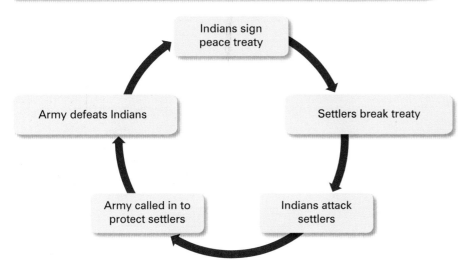

As you work through this section, try to work out how it was that millions of Indians could be controlled, have their way of life destroyed and be virtually exterminated by a much smaller force of Americans.

An elder of the Lakota Sioux said, 'They made us many promises, more than I can remember, but they only kept one; they promised to take away our land, and they took it.'

Was he right?

breech-loading rifle a gun that loads at the breech, where the gun breaks

Gatling gun an early machine gun that could fire rapidly

Ghost Dance an Indian dance that was believed to bring all dead Indians to life in order to have a final battle with the white man

Hotchkiss cannon a cannon that fired rapidly and was light enough to be used with cavalry

Indian agent an Indian appointed by the government to help run the reservations

lodge sometimes used as an alternative name for a tipi, or for a collection of tipis

muzzle-loading rifle a rifle that is loaded down through its muzzle

nomadic moving around from place to place

reservation an area designated for Indian use

scout an Indian or a soldier sent ahead of the main party to find out the lie of the land

subsidy help given in goods or money

tannery a factory where buffalo skins were made into leather

total war war in which everyone is involved – civilians as well as combatants

warpath hunting down an enemy

3.1 Conflict between settlers and Plains Indians: the Indian wars

Learning outcomes

By the end of this topic you should be able to describe, explain and understand:

● key events and misunderstandings that led to the Fort Laramie Treaties, Little Crow's War and the Sand Creek Massacre

● the reasons for Red Cloud's War and the Great Sioux War

● the role of individuals such as Red Cloud and General Custer

● the significance of the Battle of Little Big Horn as a turning point.

Activities

1 Put in chronological order the events scattered under the heading 'Getting an overview'.

2 Now fit them into the cycle of events you have drawn. As you work through this chapter, you will need to check back that you have put the events in the correct boxes, and add more events as you work through.

3 Can you suggest how this cycle could be broken?

Getting an overview

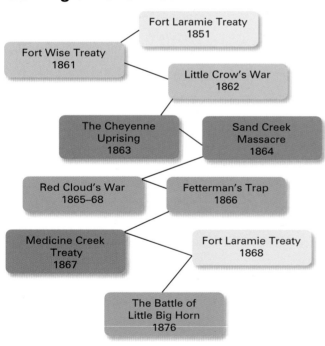

As you work through this chapter, think about:

● why US government policy changed over time

● the factors that drove this change of policy (e.g. the railroads)

● whether or not the Plains Indians could have reacted in a different way.

Government policy: the move from the 'big reservation'

Initially, as you have read, government policy was to locate all Indian tribes to the west of the 95th meridian, which became the Permanent Indian Frontier. West of that frontier, Indian tribes were free to roam and hunt at will. Or were they?

The Fort Laramie Treaty 1851

In 1849 the US government had made treaties with the Comanche and Kiowa, whereby the Indians agreed not to attack travellers on the Santa Fe Trail in return for promises of land. Thomas Fitzpatrick, a government agent, hoped to get a similar agreement with the Cheyenne and Arapaho Indians, who were attacking wagon trains along the Oregon Trail. He succeeded. The Indians agreed to the terms of the Fort Laramie Treaty, which gave them lands – they believed forever – along the foothills of the Rocky Mountains between the North Platte and Arkansas rivers. The government promised to protect them and pay the tribes $50,000 a year for ten years. In return, the Indians agreed to stop attacking travellers along the Oregon Trail, and to allow the government to build roads and military posts.

This policy became known as 'concentration' because the Indians were concentrated in specific areas. The days of one big **reservation** in the West were over; so were the days of the Permanent Indian Frontier.

The Fort Wise Treaty 1861 (later renamed the Fort Lyon Treaty)

In 1859, gold was discovered in the Rocky Mountains (see page 23).

- White men surged through the Cheyenne and Arapaho lands, forgetting about (if, indeed, they had ever known about) the agreements made with the Indians.
- Miners and other settlers moved on to Indian lands in Kansas and Nebraska.
- The railroad companies demanded the removal of buffalo and Indians from the routes along which they planned to build railroads across the Great Plains.
- In 1861, Colorado became a territory and belonged officially to white America.

Activities

1 What was the Permanent Indian Frontier? Why did the US government introduce it?

2 What pressures were the US government under to make it break the Fort Laramie Treaty?

3 Did the Fort Wise Treaty stand any chance of succeeding?

For discussion

Is the breaking of treaties ever justified?

The Cheyenne and Arapaho took their revenge. The Americans had broken the Fort Laramie Treaty, and so would they. Both Arapaho and Cheyenne began serious attacks on railroad surveyors and travellers. In 1861, the government summoned the tribal chiefs to Fort Wise and forced them to agree to abandon the terms of the Fort Laramie Treaty whereby they were given lands along the foothills of the Rockies. Instead, the government gave them a small reservation between the Arkansas River and Sand Creek in eastern Colorado.

Indian chiefs, however, had no power to force their people to do anything. Most warriors refused to accept the Fort Wise Treaty. They went on the **warpath**, raiding mining camps and attacking mail coaches in Colorado and New Mexico. The carefully worked out treaties had clearly not worked for the US government; neither had they for the Indians.

Source A: Land occupied by the Plains Indians in 1865.

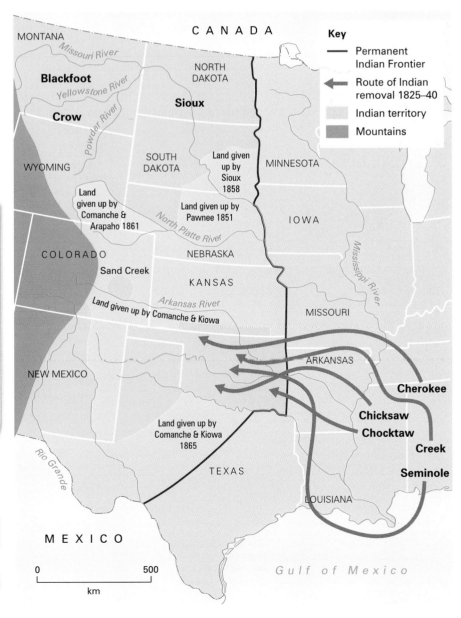

The Indian wars

It is a little difficult to talk about Indian 'wars' because Indians' ideas about warfare were very different from those of white Americans. (Look back to pages 14–16 to remind yourself what these were.) However, some 'wars' between the Indians and the US army can be identified, although there were many minor skirmishes and attacks on settlers throughout these years and many different agreements made between Indian tribes and the US government.

1 Little Crow's War 1862

Little Crow and his tribe of Santee Sioux were living on a reservation in Minnesota. In 1861, the crops failed and the compensation the Santee had been promised had not arrived from Washington, leaving the 12,000 Santee facing starvation.

In August 1862 Little Crow had had enough and led the Santee warriors in an attack on the Agency, which was the organisation set up by the government to run the reservation. The Santee took all the food and provisions from the Agency's warehouses and distributed it amongst their starving tribes-people before burning the Agency buildings to the ground. They then attacked a party of 45 US army

soldiers coming to deal with the incident, killing nearly half of them. But by October, 2,000 Santee had either been captured or had surrendered. What was left of the Santee tribe was moved to a new, smaller reservation, Crow Creek in Minnesota. The land was barren, the water unfit for drinking and food scarce. Several hundred Santee died in the first winter. One of their visitors was Sitting Bull, an important Sioux chief. What he found there affected his attitude to settlers and the US government.

2 The Sand Creek Massacre 1864

The Cheyenne, under their chief Black Kettle, faced similar problems on the Sand Creek reservation in Colorado. The starving Indians began attacking the wagon trains, that were coming into the newly opened up territory of Colorado. They took only food, leaving the travellers unharmed. After three years of raids and attacks, Black Kettle, government officials and army commanders tried to reach agreement. Believing he was under army protection, Black Kettle set up camp at Sand Creek. Meanwhile, Colonel Chivington was given responsibility for protecting settlers and dealing with the Indians. On 29 November 1864, he led a dawn raid on Black Kettle's camp at Sand Creek. There, Chivington and his men massacred over 450 men, women, children and babies, even though they were waving white flags of surrender.

Black Kettle escaped and carried news of the massacre to other tribes. Immediately the Indians increased their attacks on white people. A US Senate Committee of Enquiry, set up to enquire into

Source A: The main clashes between the Indians and the US army, 1860–90.

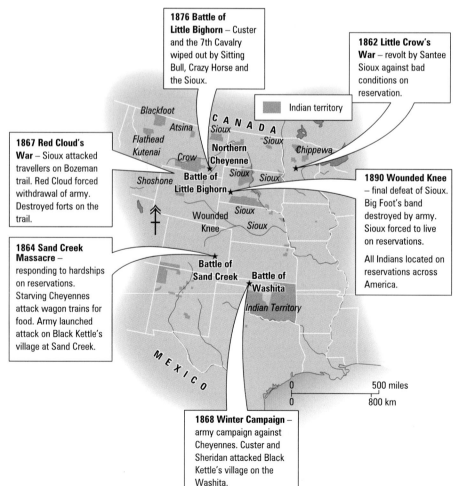

1876 Battle of Little Bighorn – Custer and the 7th Cavalry wiped out by Sitting Bull, Crazy Horse and the Sioux.

1862 Little Crow's War – revolt by Santee Sioux against bad conditions on reservation.

1867 Red Cloud's War – Sioux attacked travellers on Bozeman trail. Red Cloud forced withdrawal of army. Destroyed forts on the trail.

1864 Sand Creek Massacre – responding to hardships on reservations. Starving Cheyennes attack wagon trains for food. Army launched attack on Black Kettle's village at Sand Creek.

1890 Wounded Knee – final defeat of Sioux. Big Foot's band destroyed by army. Sioux forced to live on reservations.

All Indians located on reservations across America.

1868 Winter Campaign – army campaign against Cheyennes. Custer and Sheridan attacked Black Kettle's village on the Washita.

Indian territory

Blackfoot
Atsina
Flathead
Kutenai
Crow
Shoshone
Sioux
Northern Cheyenne
Chippewa
Battle of Little Bighorn
Wounded Knee
Battle of Sand Creek
Battle of Washita
Indian Territory
MEXICO
CANADA
Sioux

0 500 miles
0 800 km

the massacre, condemned Chivington. White men and Indians were horrified at what had happened and demanded an end to the wars. In October 1865, US government representatives met with Indian representatives at Bluff Creek, on the Arkansas River. In return for giving up their land claims and stopping violence, the Cheyenne agreed to accept money and land in Oklahoma.

3 Red Cloud's War 1865–68

The discovery of gold in Montana (see page 23) gave the government huge problems. The need for a connection between the new gold fields and the Oregon Trail led to gold miner John Bozeman establishing the Bozeman Trail. But the Bozeman Trail ran through the hunting grounds of the Sioux. This broke the Fort Laramie Treaty of 1851 (see page 76). The Indians, led by Red Cloud, Chief of the Lakota Sioux began attacking travellers along the Bozeman Trail. By 1866, the US government had had enough and set up talks with Red Cloud. At the last moment, Red Cloud discovered that the army was planning to build at least two more forts along the Bozeman trail to protect travellers. He stormed out of the meeting and the Indians kept up the pressure by attacking soldiers and other workers building the forts. Red Cloud was joined by two other equally determined Sioux leaders, Sitting Bull and Crazy Horse.

Fetterman's Trap

In December 1866. Captain William Fetterman and a group of eighty soldiers left Fort Kearney to provide protection for a wagon train bringing wood for building. They rode straight into a trap laid by the Sioux and were wiped out. Later, this was called 'Fetterman's Trap'.

The Indians surrounded Fort Kearney in a ring with armed warriors. This meant that the US army couldn't move outside the fort and no traveller could move along the Bozeman Trail. It was stalemate.

Why was Red Cloud so successful?

Red Cloud's success was that he had managed to keep together several Sioux bands as well as some of the Arapaho and Cheyenne, and he managed to keep them fighting through the winter months, a time when Indians were not accustomed to fight. By doing this he had forced the US army on to the defensive. There was much for the US government to worry about.

How was the stalemate resolved?

In March 1867, the US government set up a peace commission to try to solve the Indian problem once and for all. It was agreed that the peace treaties made with the Indians had not worked. Both Indians and white men had broken them: white people now

Source C: Indian reservations in 1875.

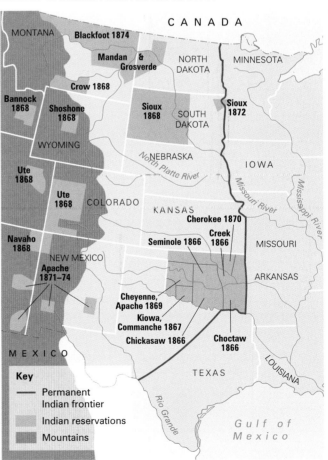

Source B: The Bozeman Trail.

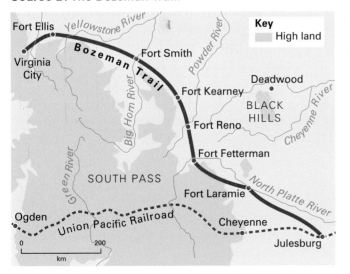

80

wanted the Plains, but so did the Indians. The US government decided that the only answer to the problem was to split the Indian tribes and to put them separately in small reservations. You can see these reservations on the map, Source B.

The Fort Laramie Treaty 1868

- The US government agreed to abandon three forts and the Bozeman Trail. (It had already found another route from the gold fields.)

- Red Cloud agreed to take his people to a reservation in Dakota, stretching from the Black Hills of Dakota to the Missouri River.

- Red Cloud was pleased with the Treaty. He believed he had won.

Were small reservations the answer?

In the summer and autumn of 1868, the government extended its 'small reservation' policy to the Rocky Mountain area. The tribes there agreed to go to small reservations scattered throughout Colorado, Idaho, Wyoming, Arizona and New Mexico.

At first it seemed that Indians and white people would be able to live together. But there was trouble ahead. Many Indians, particularly the young braves, could not settle on the reservations where their **nomadic** life was over. And no one

could suspect that the white men would soon want the Black Hills of Dakota.

The Great Sioux War 1876–77

The final, decisive battle between the whites and Indians was to begin in the Black Hills of Dakota: a sacred place for the Cheyenne, Arapaho and Sioux, and a place rich in gold. Remember that by the terms of the 1868 Fort Laramie Treaty, whites were forbidden to prospect there and Indians were not interested in gold, anyway. So all should have been well.

Why did the Sioux go back on the warpath?

Peace would hold good in the Great Sioux Reservation and the Big Horn country, where Sitting Bull and Crazy Horse still roamed free, only as long as white settlers, or would-be settlers, did not enter Indian territory.

- The Northern Pacific Railroad was fast approaching Sioux hunting grounds in Dakota, and in 1874 General George Custer led an expedition of 8th Cavalry men from Fort Abraham Lincoln to protect the railroad builders from Indian attacks. But he was not there just to protect railroad builders. He was there to look for gold, and he found it. Within six months, thousands of prospectors were swarming all over the Black Hills, staking claims to land the Sioux believed to be theirs by right and by US law. This was in clear breach of the 1868 Fort Laramie Treaty.

- The US government offered to buy the Black Hills from the Sioux for $6 million or $400,000 a year for the mineral rights. The Indians refused the offer.

- In December 1875, the government ordered the Sioux to return to their reservation. They were given 60 days to obey, after which time President Grant stated that any Indians outside the reservation should be considered hostile and could be attacked.

- Deep snows and the usual appalling winter weather made it impossible for all Indians to obey President Grant's order, even if they had wanted to. By the spring of 1876, more than 7,000 Indians, 2,000 of whom were warriors, had erected around 1,000 **lodges** on lands between the Powder River and the Rosebud River. They were ready for war.

Activities

1. How successful was Red Cloud?

2. (a) Why did the US government decide to introduce a new Indian policy in 1867?

    (b) What was new about the policy?

3. These are the words of Red Cloud:
    'Whose voice was first sounded on this land? The voice of the red people who had bows and arrows. What has been done in my country I did not want, did not ask for it; when the white man comes into my country he leaves a trail of blood behind him. I have two mountains in that country – the Black Hills and the Big Horn mountain. I want the Great Father [the US president] to make no roads through them.'
    What arguments would US government officials use against what Red Cloud was saying?

- Sitting Bull had a vision of white men falling into a Sioux camp, which he interpreted as meaning that the Sioux would have a great victory. After wiping out an army camp by the Rosebud River, Sitting Bull and Crazy Horse led their people west, towards the river that the Indians named Greasy Grass River, and that the whites called Little Big Horn.

The Battle of Little Big Horn 1876

The US Army was not discouraged by Sitting Bull's defeat of General Crook and his troops at Rosebud River on 17 June 1876. General Alfred Terry, who was in charge of this particular campaign against the Indians, did not want Sitting Bull and Crazy Horse to slip away. Thanks to his Indian **scouts**, he thought he knew where they were. He ordered Colonel John Gibbon to take a column of infantry eastwards out of Fort Ellis along the valley of the Yellowstone River to where it met the Big Horn River. They were to attack the Indian camp from the north. He ordered General Custer, with the much faster 7th Cavalry, to find and follow the Indians' trail before it went cold, locate their camp precisely, and attack it from the south in a combined effort with Gibbon's infantry.

At dawn on 25 June 1876, Custer's Indian scouts spotted the Indian camp. It was the biggest camp ever seen on the Great Plains. Despite being warned that the 7th Cavalry had not got enough bullets to kill all the Indians seen, Custer did not seem bothered: 'The largest Indian camp on the North American continent is ahead and I am going to attack it.' And he did.

Custer had 600 men and two officers, Major Marcus Reno and Captain Frederick Benteen. He used his usual tactics and split his men in order to surround the enemy. Benteen took three companies and moved west; Reno took another three companies and prepared to attack from the south. Custer and the remaining five companies aimed to attack from the north. Things went badly wrong from the start. Reno was stopped by hordes of Lakota warriors. Benteen went to help him and regrouped Reno's men, holding a hilltop but being kept there by hundreds of Indians. Custer and his men were alone and without support. They were engaged in a fight to the death. No one knows for sure what happened, but archaeological evidence suggests that they never crossed the Big Horn River. As they approached a shallow ford they were met by 1,500 Indian warriors on horseback. They retreated, fighting hard and struggling to reach higher ground and comparative safety. Just as they got there, Crazy Horse and 1,000 Oglala Sioux and Cheyenne warriors came pouring over, sweeping away everything in front of them and firing from the latest Winchester repeating rifles. Some of Custer's men may have fought bravely to the end; some may have fled in panic; others may have shot themselves to avoid mutilation. Whatever happened, it probably lasted about an hour.

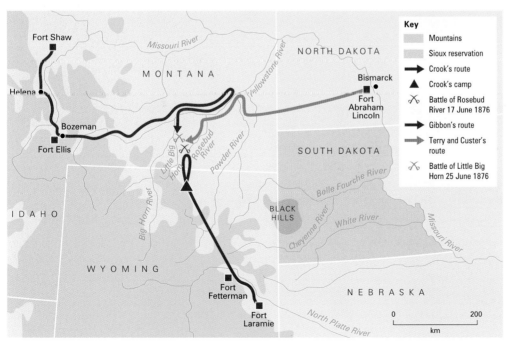

Source A: A map showing battlefields, routes taken and camps in relation to the Battle of Little Big Horn.

Late on 26 June, the Indians began to withdraw. They took down their tipis, set fire to the prairie and headed for the Big Horn mountains. Sitting Bull's vision had come true: they had won.

When Terry and his men arrived on the following day, 27 June, they found the bodies of all 225 of Custer's men. Most of them had been stripped, disfigured and scalped. Custer himself had been shot twice: though the left temple and the heart. He had not been stripped and he had not been scalped.

For discussion

Is it ever justified to disobey an order?

Challenge

Little Crow, Red Cloud and Sitting Bull were all Sioux leaders. Research their successes and failures, and reach a conclusion about who was the best leader of the Sioux nation.

Source B: A reconstruction of the Battle of Little Big Horn, painted by Edgar Paxson in 1899 after a good deal of research. Custer is in the painting, top middle.

Source C: *The Battle of Little Big Horn*, painted by Kicking Bear. This is the only painting by an eyewitness known to exist.

ResultsPlus
Build better answers

Explain the importance of the Battle of Little Big Horn in the struggle between Indians and the US army. (9 marks)

■ **Basic, Level 1 (1–3 marks)**
Answer makes undeveloped statements without details. For example, 'General Custer was killed'; 'the Indians won a great victory'.

● **Good, Level 2 (4–6 marks)**
Answer adds detail to describe what happened. For example: 'General Terry ordered Custer to attack the Indians from the south, working together with Colonel Gibbon who would attack from the north. Custer disobeyed orders and went ahead with the attack on his own.'

▲ **Excellent, Level 3 (7–9 marks)**
Answer explains the importance of the Battle of Little Big Horn, showing how, although it was a significant victory for the Indians, the impact on the USA was to harden attitudes, and therefore policy, towards managing the Indian tribes.

Activities

1 Set up a debate. One side should prepare a case for the US government needing to break the 1868 Fort Laramie Treaty. The other side should put the Sioux case for going to war to defend the Treaty. Argue it out!

2 Was General Custer to blame for the US defeat at the Battle of Little Big Horn?

3 Look at both the paintings of the Battle of Little Big Horn (Sources B and C).
   (a) What information about the battle can you find in Edgar Paxson's painting?
   (b) What information about the battle can you find in Kicking Bear's painting?
   (c) On what do the two paintings agree?

Summary

- The 1851 Fort Laramie Treaty ended the Permanent Indian Frontier and the concept of one big reservation in the West by introducing the formal policy of 'concentration', whereby Indians were concentrated in specific areas. In return for giving up their freedom to roam the Plains, Indians were given money and promised protection.

- The discovery of gold in the Rocky Mountains (1859) led to the US government permitting encroachment into Cheyenne and Arapaho lands, which resulted in the tribes going on the warpath. The Fort Wise Treaty (1861) moved the Indians to smaller reservations. Many Indians refused to accept it.

- In 1862, starving Santee Indians, led by Little Crow, attacked their reservation agency and stole food. They extended their attacks to wagon trains but again stole only food. When they were rounded up, 38 were hanged, and the rest sent to a smaller reservation in Minnesota where conditions were poor.

- In 1863, the Cheyenne faced similar problems on their Colorado reservation, which were worsened by the US government opening Colorado for settlement. The Indians attacked wagon trains, again stealing only food. US reprisals resulted in the Sand Creek Massacre, an atrocity so bad that a US Senate Committee of Enquiry was held. The Enquiry condemned Colonel Chivington who had led the massacre.

- The discovery of gold in Montana led to the development of the Bozeman Trail through the hunting grounds of the Sioux and broke the 1851 Fort Laramie Treaty. The Sioux took to the warpath. Under the terms of the 1868 Fort Laramie Treaty the US government abandoned the Bozeman Trail and three forts, and Red Kettle took his tribe to a new reservation in Dakota.

- The discovery of gold in the Black Hills of Dakota and the US government's unwillingness to stop either the miners or the fast-approaching Northern Pacific Railroad broke the 1868 Fort Laramie Treaty and set the Sioux on the warpath again. After defeating the US army at Rosebud Creek, the Sioux had an overwhelming victory at the Battle of Little Big Horn in 1876.

3.2 Change of policy from 1876: destruction of the Native American way of life

Learning outcomes

By the end of this topic you will be able to describe, explain and understand:

- the impact of the Battle of Little Big Horn in changing attitudes to the Plains Indians after 1876
- the roles of government, army and railroads in destroying the Plains Indians' way of life
- the importance of the Dawes Act.

Activities

1 What can you learn from the photograph on this page about the activities of white Americans on the Great Plains?

2 What conclusions can you draw from the photograph about the life of Indians on the Plains at that time?

Getting an overview

The main focus of this section is the process by which the Indians' way of life was destroyed. Many different methods were used; some were deliberate and some had the destruction of the Indians' way of life as an unexpected outcome.

Source A: Buffalo skulls piled beside a railroad, ready to be transported to Michigan Carbon works 1880.

The Battle of Little Big Horn: the beginning of the end of the Indians' way of life?

News of the massacre of General Custer and his men at the Battle of Little Big Horn reached most of the rest of America on 4 July – the 100th anniversary of the USA's independence from Britain – and was greeted with profound shock. You have already read (pages 81–82) about the battle itself, but how did it affect public opinion and so government reaction?

What was the impact of the Battle of Little Big Horn on public opinion?

Until Little Big Horn, public opinion had been largely behind the government policy of trying to reach agreements with the Indians. The treaties of Fort Laramie and Fort Wise, for example, showed how the government was trying to meet the needs of the Indians to hunt and roam as well as the demands of miners, settlers, ranchers and railroad builders. Little Big Horn changed all that.

How did the government and army react to the Battle of Little Big Horn?

There was enormous pressure on the US government to crush the Indians once and forever.

- Two new forts were built on the Yellowstone River.
- 2,500 army reinforcements were sent West.

- The Cheyenne and Sioux bands went their separate ways after the battle, but army divisions, led by General Crook and General Terry, pursued them relentlessly. Short of ammunition, food and supplies, by the end of 1876 most Indians had drifted back to their reservations, exhausted.
- In the spring of 1877, Crazy Horse was captured by the US army and killed in the autumn while trying to escape from Fort Robinson.
- Sitting Bull took his people to Canada, hoping for British protection. Shortage of food forced their return, where they surrendered to US government forces in 1881.

Source A: From the *Chicago Tribune*, 7 July 1876.

> It is time to quit this Sunday School policy, and let Sheridan [the Commander-in-Chief of the army in the West] recruit regiments of Western pioneer hunters and scouts, and exterminate every Indian who will not remain upon the reservations. The best use to make of an Indian who will not stay on a reservation is to kill him. It is time that the dawdling, maudlin peace-policy was abandoned.

Source B: Reputedly said by General Philip Sheridan, quoted often at the time but denied by him.

> The only good Indian is a dead Indian.

Source C: From Isabella Bird, *A Lady's Life in the Rocky Mountains*, published in 1879.

> The Americans will never solve the Indian problem until the Indian is extinct. They have treated them in a way which has intensified their treachery and devilry as enemies. The Indian Agency has been a sink of fraud and corruption; it is said that barely 30 per cent of the allowance ever reaches those for whom it is voted; and the complaints of shoddy blankets, damaged flour and worthless firearms are universal. 'To get rid of the Injuns' is the phrase used everywhere. Even their reservations do not escape seizure, for if gold is discovered on them, the Indians are moved and are compelled to accept land further west or are shot off and driven off.

- Back in their reservations, the Sioux were forced to sell the Black Hills, the Powder River Country and the Big Horn mountains. Their weapons and horses were taken from them and they had to live under military rule.

All effective resistance by the Indians on the Plains was over.

Activities

1 Read Source A. How has the *Chicago Tribune* been affected by the Battle of Little Big Horn?
2 Read Source C. How far is Isabella Bird sympathetic to the plight of the Indians?
3 Read Sources A, B and C. To what extent do all three sources agree on what should be done after the Battle of Little Big Horn?

What was the role of the army in the destruction of the Indians' way of life?

The US army and the Plains Indians were very different fighting forces, as you have seen. The Plains Indians were the guerrilla fighters of the 19th-century West – living off the land, skilled in hiding, hunting and ambushing. Their mode of fighting was to use short, sharp raids, quite unlike the US army, which was trained to fight major battles. In the 1840s and 1850s, the army in the West was relatively weak. By the mid-1850s, it consisted of some 15,715 officers and men based in 52 forts, who were responsible for keeping the peace between Indians and settlers over an area of 4 million square kilometres. Their job was made harder by the fact that most of them were in infantry regiments, not cavalry, and infantry were of little use against the excellent horsemanship of the Plains Indians.

It was by no means obvious at the start that the US army would win. So how did they do it? Superior weaponry? Tactics? Luck? You may have had some ideas already, and you may have been changing them as you have worked through this book.

How did the army use the Indians?

The Sioux nation was dominant among the Plains Indians. The US army therefore adopted a cunning tactic. They recruited spies (called scouts) from tribes hostile to the Sioux, who could be relied upon to hate the Sioux more than they hated the US army. The Shoshone and Crow Indians, for example, were particularly useful here. The scouts gave the army invaluable information about Sioux positions, battle tactics and the land over which they were fighting.

As well as helping the US army in direct ways, the fact that the Indians could not put aside their traditional differences and fight together against the army helped the US army, too. A seriously determined, united force of thousands of Indians would have presented a formidable threat to the army and just might have won. Some far-sighted leaders, such as Red Cloud, tried to get traditional enemies to fight together, but in the end he failed.

How important were forts?

The US army set up a series of forts to protect people travelling the trails and to keep watch over the Indians on reservations. The army used them as bases from which to patrol the trails and attack troublesome Indians.

Source A: A description of an army fort made by a cavalryman in 1852.

> The buildings are built from mud brick in a hollow square, leaving in the centre what is called a 'parade ground' where the military parades are held every morning. One side of the square is used as officers' quarters; the opposite side as a guard house and offices; the other two sides are soldiers' barracks. There is a flag staff in the centre from which the stars and stripes wave in the breeze.

Although the Indians attacked the forts on many occasions, such as the attack on Fort Ridgely during Little Crow's War and the attack on Fort Kearney during Red Cloud's War, they never managed to capture one. The forts took the US army deep into Indian territory – and provided them with a place of safety if they needed it.

What about weaponry?

Indians fought with their traditional weapons of bows and arrows, clubs, spears and knives. Although the Indians had guns, they were less well equipped than the army. For example, when Crazy Horse surrendered in 1877 with his 250 warriors, they had between them 46 **breech-loading rifles**, 35 **muzzle-loading rifles** and 33 revolvers. In the US army, every soldier had a rifle, and army units often had artillery and **Gatling guns** (an early type of machine gun).

How did the army's tactics help them to win?

Two of the most successful generals in the Civil War (1861–65) were William Sherman and Philip Sheridan. Once the Civil War was over, they turned their attention to the Plains Indians, and introduced new tactics:

- **Total war** involved a change of attitude. War was to be waged against all Sioux – women, children and old men as well as braves. The Indians were not attacked directly, but their tipis, clothing, belongings and animals were all destroyed. The Sioux then had to make a choice: starve on the Plains or enter the reservations.
- **Winter campaigns** were new and very successful. The Indians were at their most vulnerable in winter. Heavy snows and sub-zero temperatures meant the bands could not move. Defeat at this time would be devastating. The US army, well fed and sheltered in their forts, began a series of winter campaigns. The army used the railroads to get close to Indian camps, and in this way got round the problems with the weather.

It was a combination of these factors that enabled the US army eventually to defeat the Plains Indians militarily. But it needed more than military defeat to change the Indians' way of life forever.

Activities

1 What problems did the US army face when fighting the Plains Indians?

2 Make a list of the factors that led to the US army successfully defeating the Plains Indians. Construct a spider diagram, showing how they were interlinked to bring about the Indians' defeat.

What was the role of the railroads in the destruction of the Indians' way of life?

The railroads played a central role in the destruction of the Indians and their way of life. The actual building of the railroads hit the Plains Indians hard, and then what the railroads brought on to the Plains completed the destruction of their way of life.

The railroads have been cropping up throughout this book and you will have read about them in nearly every section. This section aims to enable you to pull together what you already know, and to turn it round so that it focuses on the impact the railroads had on the way of life of the Indians.

- Railroads crossed the traditional hunting grounds of the Plains Indians.
- The US army protected the railroad builders from attacks by Indians.
- The railroads brought homesteaders onto the Plains.
- Cowboys took cattle on long drives across the Plains to the railheads.
- Railroads took cattle to the cities in the east of the USA, increasing demand and encouraging the development of ranching on the Plains.

- Railroads enabled soldiers and their equipment to be moved quickly over the Plains.
- Tourists were brought on to the Plains by railroad for buffalo hunts.
- Railroads helped Americans fulfil their manifest destiny.

Activities

1 Look at each of the eight bullet points describing the impact of railroads upon the Plains Indians. Working in pairs, for each bullet point, find ONE example in the book to illustrate it. Compare what you have found with others in your class, and so build up a class dossier on the ways in which the railroads helped destroy the Plains Indians' way of life.

2 Look carefully at Source A. What connections can you make between what you can see in the photograph and the destruction of the Indians' way of life?

For discussion

Could the Indians have done anything to reduce the impact of the railways on their way of life?

Source A: A photograph of General Custer with his Indian scouts in the early 1870s, guarding the building of the Northern Pacific Railroad.

How did the government help destroy the Indians' way of life?

The idea underpinning most government action within this period was that of 'manifest destiny'. In this the Plains Indians were to have no part – no part, that is, unless they were prepared to change their way of life and live like white Americans.

You have seen how, in the early days, the US government tried to work with the Plains Indians through the treaties they made with them. Each time, however, the treaties were broken because of pressure from miners and would-be settlers, railroad builders and, most importantly, the army. The government backed the US army in the tactics it used to make the Plains safe for settlers, and, of course, paid officers and men and made funds available for the purchase of guns and bullets, uniforms and equipment. It was the government that thought up and supported the policy of putting as many Indians as possible into reservations – and this policy was stepped up, particularly after the Battle of Little Big Horn. Not only were more and more Indians forced into reservations, but the Indians' way of life was destroyed within them (you will read more about this in Section 3.3) and the reservations themselves were made smaller and smaller.

Source A: Part of a speech made by US President Chester A. Arthur on 6 December 1881.

> The allotment system will have a direct and powerful influence in dissolving the tribal band, which is so prominent a feature of savage life, and which tends so prominently to perpetuate [maintain] it.

The Dawes Act 1887

The Dawes General Allotment Act was passed in 1887. It was a result of the general belief that, if Indians were ever to behave like white men, they had to be given land to farm.

- The Act divided the Indian reservations into farms of 160 acres for each adult and 80 acres for each child in a family.
- Any land left over was to be sold to white settlers.

Source B: Maps showing the reduction of the Great Sioux Reservation 1863–89.

Treaty of 1863

Agreement of 1875

Act of 1889

Key
Great Sioux Reservation

It was quite clear what the US government had in mind.

However, the problem was that many Indians would not accept the land. Many of those who did accept land sold it back to white men as soon as they could, for pitifully small amounts of money. Unhappy with the land they had to farm, or landless because they had sold their allocation to the first bidder, more and more Indians were forced to become dependent on white people to feed them and give them shelter. The reservations were gone, divided between Indians and whites who were prepared to farm the land. What, now, would happen to the Indian territory?

The Oklahoma land race 1889

The answer was simple: it was to be opened up to white settlers. On 23 March 1889, President Harrison announced that 2 million acres in the former Indian Territory of Oklahoma would soon be opened up to settlers. Thousands of hopeful settlers gathered on the edge of the unopened territory, and on 22 April bugles, guns and flags told them they could cross the boundary. Across they rushed, hundreds of them on horseback and in wagons. In 1893, a further 6 million acres were opened up for settlement. Almost 60 years earlier, this land had been promised to the Cherokee Indians for ever.

Activities

1 Make a list of the pressures on the government to favour white Americans over the Indians.

2 How far was the Battle of Little Big Horn a turning point in the treatment of the Plains Indians?

3 What does Source B tell you about attitudes to the Indians and to their land?

Source C: *The run* painted by John Noble shows the dash for land in Oklahoma, 22 April 1889.

Challenge

Consider the three agents of change: the army, the railroads and the government. Which was the more important in bringing about change? You will need to weigh the evidence and reach a supported judgement. It may help you to sketch out a spider diagram, showing how they were all connected, to help you plan your answer.

For discussion

Do you think the government deliberately tried to destroy the Plains Indians' way of life?

Summary

- The impact of the Battle of Little Big Horn on the USA was one of profound shock. Public opinion began to turn against the Indians. The government responded by reinforcing the army, forcing the Indians back into their reservations and forcibly buying from them the Black Hills, the Powder River Country and the Big Horn mountains.

- The US army played an important role in the destruction of the Plains Indians' way of life. Their forts took them deep into Indian territory, and the army used the forts as bases from which to protect settlers, travellers and miners, which involved attacking Indians. The army used Indians as scouts, taking care to select them from tribes that were traditional enemies of the Sioux, who were the largest Indian nation on the Plains. A change of tactics to total war and winter campaigns ensured the military defeat of the Indians.

- The railroads played a central role in the destruction of the Indian way of life. The building of the railroads disturbed their traditional hunting grounds, and the development of the cattle industry on the Plains was dependent on the railroads. The railroads brought settlers and tourists, machinery and supplies on to the Plains and took the produce of the homesteaders back to cities in the East.

- The government supported Americans wanting to cross the Plains and settle and work on them. In doing so, it backed the army's strategy and tactics. Although initially the government tried to reach agreements with the Indians, these were constantly broken as the US government came under more and more pressure to exploit Indian land. The policy of 'encouraging' Indians into reservations was continued and extended, until the Dawes Act (1887) divided the reservation land into parcels for farming, an occupation alien to the Indian way of life. The remaining Indian Territory (Oklahoma) was opened up for settlement in 1889. Manifest destiny had been fulfilled.

3.3 Changes to Native American culture by 1890: life on reservations

Learning outcomes

By the end of this topic you will be able to describe, explain and understand:

● the ways in which government control of life on the reservations destroyed the Plains Indians' culture

● the impact of the destruction of the buffalo herds on the Plains Indians' culture and whether or not this was deliberate government policy

● the significance of the Ghost Dance and the Battle of Wounded Knee in demonstrating
the end of the way of life of Indians on the Great Plains.

Getting an overview

It was over. The white man had won the struggle for the Plains. The Indians had been cleared from their hunting grounds. There was then, as you have seen, nothing to stop white people from claiming and settling all the land. They could put it to the plough, grow crops and use the land as they believed it should be used. The dream of 'manifest destiny' had been fulfilled. But what of the Indians? The US government had to be sure they could be controlled.

Activities

1 What evidence can you find in the photograph of the survival of the Indians' traditional way of life?

2 What can you learn from the photograph about the ways in which the traditional life of the Sioux Indians had been destroyed?

3 How would a government supporter use this photograph as evidence that the Sioux were being controlled by the government?

Source A: A photograph showing government agents distributing food rations on a Sioux reservation.

How were the reservations used to control the Indians?

In 1825, the US government began developing a system of reservations on the Great Plains. Reservations were intended to keep the Indians away from the homesteaders and ranchers. Once on the reservations, the Indians were expected to farm the land, though they were, in the early days, allowed to leave to hunt the buffalo. Government-appointed **Indian agents** saw that the reservations were run properly.

Taking away the power of the tribal chiefs

In 1871, the US government decided that no more treaties should be signed with tribal chiefs. In the early 1880s, it set up special councils among the tribes. These councils were to take over the chiefs' powers that had enabled them to look after their people on the reservations. In 1883, special courts took over the chiefs' powers to judge and punish the Indians. In 1885, however, these courts were abolished. In future, the US federal law courts would keep law and order among the Indians on their reservations and punish any wrongdoers. The Indians had lost all ability to govern themselves.

Taking away their children

Children were the future of the tribe. Taught the tribes' traditions and way of life, they would continue to keep the tribe alive down through future generations. But the US government put a stop to that. The children – boys and girls – were taken off the reservations and sent to school. No Indian tribe, and no Indian parent, wanted their children treated in this way, but if they resisted or refused, their food rations were withdrawn until they agreed. Once in school, the children lived and learned under military-style conditions. Punished if they spoke their own language, they were taught to have no respect for their traditional way of life. By 1887, 2,020 Indian children were pupils at 117 boarding schools and 2,500 were in 110 day schools. One boarding school founder said that his aim was to 'kill the Indian in him and save the man'. When the children returned to their reservations, they found that they could not fit in with the Indian way of life, nor with the way of life of white America. They were aliens to both cultures.

Activities

1 Look at Source A and at the changes between the two photographs. Work in threes. One of you has to get into the shoes of the boys, one into the shoes of the school's head teacher and one into the shoes of the boys' parents. What do you feel about the changes? Make notes about what you would feel, and why. Then act it out as a conversation.

Source A: Two photographs of the same three Sioux boys. The one on the left was taken when they arrived at the Carlisle Indian School in Pennsylvania. The one on the right was taken six months later.

Taking away their skills

The Indians had lost the power to govern themselves and their children. They had also lost their skills. The Sioux were particularly badly hit. They could not roam the Great Plains and they could not hunt; the buffalo were gone and so were their horses. The economic foundations of their society had been destroyed. There was no buffalo meat for food, no buffalo hide for tipis and no chance of stealing horses. They were expected to turn themselves into farmers, but the skills they had were the skills of hunting and fighting, not ploughing, sowing and reaping. For Indian nations such as the Pawnee, the change was not so dramatic because they were farmers as well as hunters. Even so, all the reservations were mostly on poor land and did not farm well. Gradually, the Indians became dependent on government handouts to keep them from starvation.

Taking away their religion

The US government banned all Indian feasts, dances and ceremonies on the reservations. This was later to cause trouble (see page 96). The banning of ceremonies undermined the power of the medicine man in the tribe: no longer was there any point in young men seeking visions or any need to search for the buffalo. This spiritual gap was filled by the arrival on the reservations of Christian missionaries, with the aim of 'civilising' the Indians.

Source B: A Kiowa Indian, Wohaw, painted this picture called *The Red Man's Dilemma*.

The role of government agents

Government agents, who were supposed to be looking after the interests of the reservation Indians, were frequently corrupt or, at the very least, ran scams on the side. Housing **subsidies** vanished; rations were inadequate and medical provision non-existent. Measles and influenza were rife on the reservations and were killer diseases. All this added to the depressing and demoralising nature of the lives led by the Indians.

The Sioux Chief Sitting Bull refused to cooperate with Indian agents, but lesser chiefs gained importance (if only in the eyes of the government) by doing so. They also gained concessions such as increased food rations and better medical supplies. A number of Indians joined the Indian Agency Police where they were fed, clothed and sheltered and were generally able to maintain a reasonable standard of living.

Activities

2 You are an investigative journalist in 1895. Your editor has sent you to a Sioux reservation to report on conditions there. You must decide whether you are pro or anti government policy. Make your report as sensational as you can!

Source C: Members of the Indian Agency Police at the Standing Rock Agency.

For discussion

Look at Source B. What was the Red Man's dilemma? Did the Indians really have a choice?

Control by the destruction of the buffalo?

It has been estimated that in 1840 there were around 13 million buffalo roaming the Great Plains. They were central to the Indians' way of life and to their survival (see pages 8–9). Yet by 1885 there were only about 200 buffalo left, and the Indians were forced into reservations if they were to survive. How had destruction on such a scale happened?

Were the railroads to blame?

Railroads brought tourists in special excursion trains on to the Great Plains especially to shoot buffalo for sport (see pages 52–53). Buffalo hunters were employed by the railroad companies to kill buffalo in order to keep their construction workers supplied with fresh meat. One of these buffalo hunters was William Cody, nicknamed Buffalo Bill for his skill at killing. The Kansas Pacific Railroad Company paid him $500 a month to clear buffalo from the tracks and supply the workers with fresh meat daily. He claimed he killed 4,280 buffalo in 17 months.

Was industry to blame?

In 1871, a **tannery** in the eastern states invented a process whereby high-grade leather could be made from buffalo hides. The price of buffalo hides shot up, and thousands and thousands of animals were killed. Train load after train load of hides were transported east as the numbers of white hunters increased dramatically. The industry was centred on Dodge City and Fort Worth, and therefore the hunters focused on the southern herd. In a desperate attempt to save the buffalo and their own way of life, in the summer of 1874 some 700 Arapaho, Cheyenne, Comanche and Kiowa launched an attack on buffalo hunters based near Adobe Walls on the western edge of the southern herd. They failed. By the end of 1875, the southern herd was destroyed.

The destruction of the northern herd did not begin until 1880. The Northern Pacific Railroad reached Bismarck in 1876, the Sioux were defeated in the wars of 1876–77, and then the killing of the buffalo began. By 1882, an estimated 5,000 skinners and hunters were at work. By 1883, the northern herd had been exterminated.

Source A: A map of the Great Plains, showing the main railroads and the southern and northern buffalo herds. The railroads split the one great herd into two.

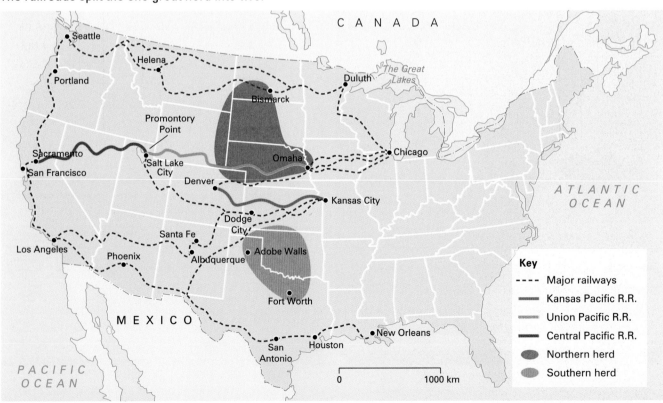

Who was behind the buffalo slaughter?

Clearly one of the reasons for the slaughter of the buffalo was simple greed. But was there anything else going on? When the US government first set up reservations for Indians (see page 76), the Indians were allowed to leave them to hunt buffalo. However, by the late 1860s US government policy had changed. Indians on reservations had to learn to live like white people and so were forbidden to follow their traditions – and this included buffalo hunting. To remove the buffalo would mean that there would be little point in the Indians protesting and this would make them easier to control.

Source B: Part of a speech made by General Philip Sheridan to the Texas legislature in 1873.

> These men [the buffalo hunters] have done more in the last two years, and will do more in the next year, to settle the vexed Indian question, than the entire regular army has done in the last 30 years. They are destroying the Indians' food supply. For the sake of a lasting peace, let them kill, skin and sell until the buffalos are exterminated.

Source C: Comments made by Frank H. Mayer, a buffalo hunter based in Dodge City in 1873. He remembers what happened when he rode into army camps and was given as much ammunition as he wanted.

> I asked an officer, 'What am I expected to do with this ammunition – kill Indians?' 'Hell no, that's our job,' replied the officer. 'You just kill buffalo. We'll take care of the Indians. Either the buffalo or the Indians must go. There isn't any other way. Only when the Indian becomes absolutely dependent on us for his every need, will we be able to handle him. Every buffalo you kill will save a white man's life. Go to it.'

Source D: Comments made by a cowboy Teddy 'Blue' Abbott, in the 1880s.

> The buffalo slaughter was a dirty business. All this slaughter was a put-up job on the part of the government to control Indians by getting rid of their food supply. But just the same, it was a low-down, dirty business.

Source E: From Richard White *The Oxford History of the American West*, published in 1994.

> It now appears that the buffalo was in trouble by the 1840s not so much from over-hunting, although this was a factor, but from a combination of drought, destruction of its habitat by white settlers, competition for grass with Indian horse herds and diseases brought by the cattle of white travellers.

Activities

1 Plains Indians and white men both hunted the buffalo. What were (a) the similarities and (b) the differences between their methods and their motives?

2 Read Source B. General Sheridan was an army man. Are you surprised by what he said?

3 Read Sources C and D. How far do they agree about the killing of the buffalo?

4 Do you agree with Teddy 'Blue' Abbott when he says that the slaughter of the buffalo was a put-up job by the government to control the Indians?

5 Now read Source E. Explain whether or not it makes you change your mind about the answers you gave to activities 2–4.

For discussion

How significant were the railroads in the destruction of the buffalo?

The Battle of Wounded Knee: the final tragedy

By the end of the 1880s, the atmosphere among Indians on the reservations was one of disillusionment and despair. This was heightened by a government-imposed cut in Sioux rations coupled with a drought in the summer of 1890 that led to a failure of Sioux crops. Into this grim situation came the **Ghost Dance**.

What was the importance of the Ghost Dance?

A Paiute Indian, Wovoka, claimed to have had a vision telling him that all Indians everywhere had to dance, dance and keep on dancing. The Great Spirit would then bring all the dead Indians back to life, a great flood would carry away the white people, and the land would belong to the Indians again. The Ghost Dance spread like a prairie fire through the reservations. The Indian agents were worried – and became even more worried when some dancers in some reservations danced with rifles held above their heads. US President Harrison ordered the army into the reservations to take control. Chief Sitting Bull, one of the chiefs supporting the Ghost Dance, was killed in a botched attempt to arrest him. He was shot dead by one of his own tribe – a Sioux policeman.

The Battle of Wounded Knee (29 December 1890)

Sitting Bull's followers fled south to join the band of Big Foot in the Cheyenne River Reservation. But the US army were moving to arrest Big Foot, too, who had fled with his band of 120 men and 230 women and children. Hampered by deep December snows, and suffering from pneumonia, the Indians were in a bad way when the 7th Cavalry caught up with them. The Indians were taken under armed guard to Wounded Knee Creek, where the army began to disarm them. At least one Sioux warrior resisted and others began to dance. In the general confusion, a shot rang out and the 7th Cavalry opened fire with repeating rifles and **Hotchkiss cannon**. The Indians fought back with what weapons they had, but they did not stand a chance. Shells burst among them, tearing braves, women and children to pieces. It was all over in ten minutes. A total of 250 Indians and 25 soldiers lay dead. Private Jesse Harris said, 'Afterwards, I heard remarks from the older soldiers "This is where we got even for the Battle of Little Big Horn."' Whether it was or not, the struggle for the Plains was over.

Black Elk, Holy Man of the Oglala Sioux, should have the last word. In 1931, talking to the author John Neihardt, he said: 'I did not know then how much was ended. When I look back now from this high hill of my old age, I can still see the butchered women and children lying heaped and scattered all along the crooked gulch as plain as when I saw them with eyes still young. And I can see that something else died there in the bloody mud, and was buried in the blizzard. A people's dream died there. It was a beautiful dream. The nation's hoop is broken and scattered. There is no centre any longer and the sacred tree is dead.'

Activities

1 Reflect on the Battle of Little Big Horn and on what happened between that battle and the Battle of Wounded Knee. Would you agree that the Battle of Little Big Horn marked a turning point in attitudes to, and the treatment of, the Indians?

2 Was the destruction of the Plains Indians' way of life inevitable?

For discussion

Some soldiers said of the Battle of Wounded Knee 'This is where we got even for the Battle of Little Big Horn.' Do you agree with them?

Challenge

Use the information in this section to explain whether or not you agree with what Dee Brown says in Source B.

Source A: Big Foot lying dead, frozen in the snow, on the Wounded Knee battlefield. It was not until 3 January 1891 that the army finally collected the bodies of the Indians and buried them in a mass grave.

Source B: From Dee Brown *Bury My Heart at Wounded Knee*, published in 1971.

To justify the breaches of the Permanent Frontier, the policy makers in Washington invented 'manifest destiny'. The Europeans and their descendants were ordained by destiny to rule all of America. They were the dominant race, and therefore responsible for the Indians – along with their lands, their forests and their mineral wealth.

Summary

- The reservations were used to control the Indians. The power of the chiefs was taken away; the children were sent away to school to be educated in the ways of white people; ceremonies were banned and so medicine men lost their power; and the Indians themselves were deskilled as the buffalo were dead and they were expected to live and work as farmers. Government agents ran the reservations and they were frequently corrupt. Some Indians joined the Agency Police where they had better living and working conditions.

- The great herds of buffalo were wiped out. Professional buffalo hunters killed thousands for the tanneries and factories back in the eastern states, and thousands more were killed by tourists. This played into the government's hands as a lack of buffalo meant the Indians could not hunt and had to stay on the reservations.

- Indians on the reservations began dancing the Ghost Dance, which for them signified the coming of the end of the white man on the Plains. This worried the government, and the army was sent in to take control. Sitting Bull was killed and his followers fled to join Big Foot. Hunted by the 7th Cavalry, Big Foot and his Indians were finally gunned down in Wounded Knee Creek. That was the end of Indian resistance on the Plains.

Quick quiz

1 *Chronology quiz:* put these events in chronological order:

- destruction of the northern buffalo herd
- Battle of Little Big Horn
- Dawes Act
- the first Fort Laramie Treaty
- Red Cloud's War
- the Oklahoma land race
- Fort Wise Treaty
- Battle of Wounded Knee
- destruction of the southern buffalo herd
- discovery of gold in the Colorado Mountains

2 *Causes, events and consequences:* these causes, events, dates and consequences have been muddled up. See if you can sort them out so that each event has a correct cause, a correct date and a correct consequence.

Cause	Event	Date	Consequence
Discovery of gold in Colorado mountains led to prospectors surging through Cheyenne and Arapaho lands	Fort Laramie Treaty	1890	Indians moved to a reservation in the foothills of the Rocky Mountains, accepted money and government protection in return for stopping attacks on wagon trains and allowing government to build roads and military forts
Gold discovered in Black Hills of Dakota and prospectors staking claims on Sioux hunting grounds	Little Crow's War	1876	Pressure on the US government to crush the Plains Indians once and for all
Comanche and Kiowa Indians attacking travellers on the Santa Fe Trail	Fort Wise Treaty	1851	Indians forced to abandon terms of Fort Laramie Treaty and move to small reservation between Arkansas River and Sand Creek in eastern Colorado
The Ghost Dance inspired Indians on the reservations to believe they could win back the Plains	Sand Creek Massacre	1861	US government agreed to army abandoning three forts and gave Indians a reservation stretching from the Black Hills of Dakota to the Missouri River
Cheyenne attacking wagon trains for food	Red Cloud's War	1864	Indians moved to a smaller, worse reservation
Travellers to the gold fields of Montana attacked by Lakota Sioux on the Bozeman Trail	The Battle of Little Big Horn	1865–68	The end of the struggle for the Plains, with complete victory for the US government
Santee Sioux starving in their reservation	The Battle of Wounded Knee	1862	Indians given money and moved to smaller reservations

Revision activity

3 How did it happen?

How was it that, in the space of 50 years, white Americans were able to take over the Great Plains, and in doing so end the Indians' way of life forever? Complete the grid below. For each factor, write a sentence explaining how it brought about change, and then give it a star rating out of five to show its importance to the change where five stars = most important. There is room for you to add two (or more) factors of your own

Factor	Reason	Star rating
Manifest destiny		
US government policy		
US army		
Homesteaders		
Cattle ranching		
Gold		
Railroads		
Destruction of the buffalo		
Indian weaponry		
Indian strategy and tactics		
Reservations		

Discuss your decisions with the rest of your class and try to reach a whole class decision about what the most important reasons were for the white American take-over of the Great Plains.

Checklist

How well do you know and understand:

- events and misunderstandings that led to the Fort Laramie Treaties and the Fort Wise Treaty

- the reasons for Red Cloud's War and the Great Sioux War

- the parts played by Red Cloud and General Custer

- the significance of the Battle of Little Big Horn as a turning point in attitudes to, and actions against, the Plains Indians

- the roles of the government, army and railroads in destroying the Plains Indians' way of life

- the importance of the Dawes Act

- the ways in which the US government controlled the Plains Indians in the reservations

- the reasons why the southern and northern herds of buffalo were destroyed

- the impact of the destruction of the buffalo on the way of life of the Plains Indians

- the significance of the Ghost Dance and the Battle of Wounded Knee?

Student tip

Quite often students confuse the various battles. It is important to remember that, after two of them, the Indians believed they had won. These two were Red Cloud's War and the Battle of Little Big Horn.

What happened on the Great Plains?

The shaded areas show the periods of greatest activity in the Great Plains of each group.

| 1840 | 1850 | 1860 |

Indians
lived on the Great Plains

1840
US government says that Great Plains are Indian territory

1851
Fort Laramie Treaty (1)

1861
Fort Lyon Treaty

Early settlers
crossed the Great Plains

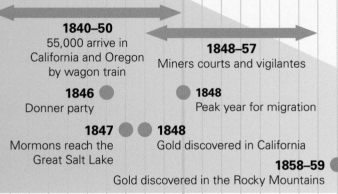

1840–50
55,000 arrive in California and Oregon by wagon train

1848–57
Miners courts and vigilantes

1846
Donner party

1848
Peak year for migration

1847
Mormons reach the Great Salt Lake

1848
Gold discovered in California

1858–59
Gold discovered in the Rocky Mountains

Cattlemen and cowboys
worked on the Great Plains

Trails blazed from Texas to New Orleans, Ohio, Chicago, California

Homesteaders
lived and worked on the Great Plains

18
Homestead A

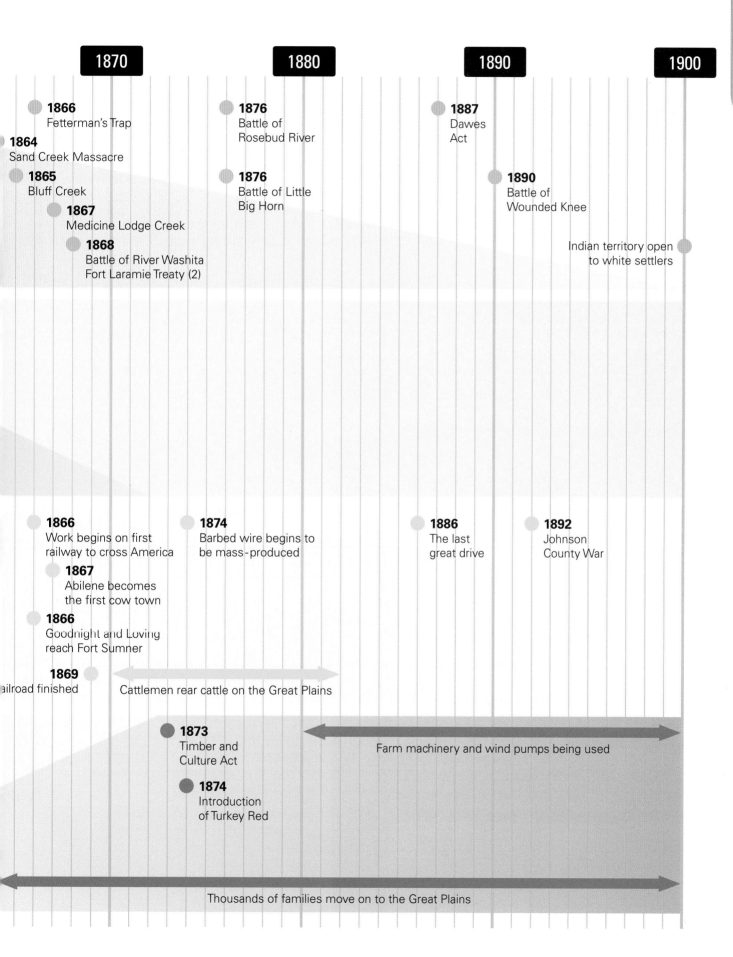

1870 **1880** **1890** **1900**

1866
Fetterman's Trap

1864
Sand Creek Massacre

1865
Bluff Creek

1867
Medicine Lodge Creek

1868
Battle of River Washita
Fort Laramie Treaty (2)

1876
Battle of
Rosebud River

1876
Battle of Little
Big Horn

1887
Dawes
Act

1890
Battle of
Wounded Knee

Indian territory open
to white settlers

1866
Work begins on first
railway to cross America

1867
Abilene becomes
the first cow town

1866
Goodnight and Loving
reach Fort Sumner

1869
ailroad finished

1874
Barbed wire begins to
be mass-produced

1886
The last
great drive

1892
Johnson
County War

Cattlemen rear cattle on the Great Plains

1873
Timber and
Culture Act

1874
Introduction
of Turkey Red

Farm machinery and wind pumps being used

Thousands of families move on to the Great Plains

Welcome to exam zone

Revising for your exams can be a daunting prospect. In this part of the book we'll take you through the best way of revising for your exams, step by step, to ensure you get the best results possible.

Zone In!

Have you ever become so absorbed in a task that suddenly it feels entirely natural and easy to perform? This is a feeling familiar to many athletes and performers. They work hard to recreate it in competition in order to do their very best. It's a feeling of being 'in the zone', and if you can achieve that same feeling in an examination, the chances are you'll perform brilliantly.

The good news is that you can get 'in the zone' by taking some simple steps in advance of the exam. Here are our top tips.

UNDERSTAND IT

Make sure you understand the exam process and what revision you need to do. This will give you confidence and also help you to get things into proportion. These pages are a good place to find some starting pointers for performing well in exams.

FRIENDS AND FAMILY

Make sure that your friends and family know when you want to revise. Even share your revision plan with them. Learn to control your times with them, so you don't get distracted. This means you can have better quality time with them when you aren't revising, because you aren't worrying about what you ought to be doing.

DEAL WITH DISTRACTIONS

Think about the issues in your life that may interfere with revision. Write them all down. Then think about how you can deal with each so they don't affect your revision.

COMPARTMENTALISE

You might not be able to deal with all the issues that can distract you. For example, you may be worried about a friend who is ill, or just be afraid of the exam. In this case, there is still a useful technique you can use. Put all of these worries into an imagined box in your mind at the start of your revision (or in the exam) and mentally lock it. Only open it again at the end of your revision session (or exam).

DIET AND EXERCISE

Make sure you eat sensibly and exercise as well! If your body is not in the right state, how can your mind be? A substantial breakfast will set you up for the day, and a light evening meal will keep your energy levels high.

BUILD CONFIDENCE

Use your revision time not only to revise content, but also to build your confidence in readiness for tackling the examination. For example, try tackling a short sequence of easy tasks in record time.

Planning Zone

The key to success in exams and revision often lies in good planning. Knowing **what** you need to do and **when** you need to do it is your best path to a stress-free experience. Here are some top tips in creating a great personal revision plan.

First of all, **know your strengths and weaknesses**.

Go through each topic making a list of how well you think you know the topic. Use your mock examination results and/or any other test results that are available as a check on your self-assessment. This will help you to plan your personal revision effectively, putting extra time into your weaker areas.

Next, *create your plan!*

Remember to make time for considering how topics interrelate.

For example, in History you will be expected to know not just what happened, but why it happened, how important it was and how one event relates to another.

The specification quite clearly states when you are expected to be able to link one topic to another, so plan this into your revision sessions.

You will be tested on this in the exam and you can gain valuable marks by showing your ability to do this.

Finally, *follow the plan!*

You can use the revision sections in the following pages to kick-start your revision.

MAY

SUNDAY	MONDAY	TUES
	30	1

Be realistic about how much time you can devote to your revision, but also make sure you put in enough time. Give yourself regular breaks or different activities to give your life some variety. Revision need not be a prison sentence!

Find out your exam dates. Go to the Edexcel website to find all final exam dates, and check with your teacher.

view Sectio
complete t
ractice exa
question

7

8

Chunk your revision in each subject down into smaller sections. This will make it more manageable and less daunting.

Draw up a list of all the dates from the start of your revision right through to your exams.

13

Review Sectio
Complete three
practice exam

20

Review Sectio
Try the Keywo
Quiz again

Make sure you allow time for assessing your progress against your initial self-assessment. Measuring progress will allow you to see and be encouraged by your improvement. These little victories will build your confidence.

22

EXAM DAY!

27

28

In the exam you will have 1 hour and 15 minutes to answer 5 questions.

- In Section A you have to answer questions 1 (4 marks) and 2 (9 marks). You will then have a choice between question 3 (12 marks) or question 4 (12 marks).

- In Section B you have a choice between questions 5 and 6, each worth 25 marks. These questions are in two parts: (a) 9 marks; and (b) 16 marks.

You can see that it is important to spend your time wisely – do not waste time on the 4-mark question in section A and then leave yourself less time for the higher-mark question at the end. Allow yourself roughly 1.5 minutes a mark. So for example, 6 minutes into the examination, you should be finished with question 1. It is also important to read each question carefully to make sure that you understand what the question is asking. Do not launch straight into an answer. When making your choices for questions 3 or 4 and 5 or 6, make sure that you understand what the question is asking you to do before you make up your mind. It is far better to spend a bit of time doing this rather than to start writing and then discover that you would be able to answer the other question better! Let's have a look at an example.

This is in capital letters because it is really important that you remember to give two things and not just one.

This question is worth only 4 marks. This means that you should spend no more than 6 minutes on it – do not waste time that you might need later by going into too much detail! Two sentences are all you need to write.

You will always be given a choice for this question.

Mini exam paper
Section A

1 Study Source A.

Source A: A painting of a cowboy in Montana, by W.H.D. Koener.

Give **TWO** things that can you learn about the work of a cowboy from Source A. (4 marks)

2 The boxes below show two important individuals and their work.

Choose **ONE** and explain the importance of his work for the growth of the cattle industry. (9 marks)

Charles Goodnight and cattle trails	Joseph McCoy and Abilene

You will always be given a source in question 1. Make sure you study it carefully as you will need to use it to answer the question. Whatever you mention must be in the source and **not** just come from your own knowledge.

It's really important that you DO NOT just write everything you know about one of these. You need to concentrate on what the question asks you – underline the key word in the question. In this case the examiner wants to know what the individual contributed to the growth of the cattle industry.

Note the key words in this question (law and order, and mining towns) and the dates. You will not get credit for any information you put that is outside this period.

These questions are worth 12 marks, so it is important that you spend quite a while on them (about 18 minutes). You might want to jot down a few ideas before you write.

Note that Question 6 is not included here but will be the same question type as Question 5. You may choose one or the other.

Pick out the key words in the questions. In this case they are 'describe the difficulties' and 'travelling west by wagon trains in the 1840s'. Many students lose marks because they do not read the questions properly.

Take note of the years in all questions. Any information you write that is outside the period will not gain you any marks.

Again, this is here for a reason – to help you! Do not ignore it. On the other hand if you have more information, it is important that you write it in your answer as you will not be able to get excellent marks using this information alone.

Answer **EITHER** Question 3 **OR** Question 4

EITHER

3 Why were there problems of law and order in the mining towns in the Far West in the 1850s and 1860s? (12 marks)

> You may use the following in your answer and any other information of your own.
> - At least 90,000 single men arrived in California in 1849.
> - Miners set up their own courts of law.
> - In 1853, San Francisco had 537 saloons.

Section A total = 25 marks

Section B

Answer **EITHER** Question 5 **OR** Question 6

You must answer both parts of the question you choose.

EITHER

5 (a) Describe the difficulties faced by the early migrants travelling west by wagon trains in the 1840s. (9 marks)

(b) 'The leadership of Brigham Young was the most important reason for the success of the Mormons in establishing a settlement at Salt Lake City'. Do you agree with this statement? Explain your answer. (16 marks)

> You may use the following in your answer and any other information of your own.
> - The Church allocated land to each family.
> - The Mormons asked for an independent state called Deseret in 1848.
> - The Perpetual Emigration Fund was set up in 1854.

Section B total = 25 marks

Note that Question 4 is not included here but will be the same question type as Question 3. You may choose one or the other.

This information is here to help you! This means that these three will be relevant to the question. You do not have to use any of the bullet points, and you will not lose marks for leaving any of them out, but you should mention them if you can. It does not mean that is all you need to write though – if you can think of other reasons then add those, too.

These directions are important. Make sure that you read all four questions **and** that you can answer both parts of the question before you make your choice. Remember that question (b) carries the most marks.

This question is worth a lot of marks! Make sure that you leave enough time for it – around 24 minutes.

Why were there problems of law and order in the mining towns in the Far West in the 1850s and 1860s? (12 marks)

You may use the following in your answer and any other information of your own.
- At least 90,000 single men arrived in California in 1849.
- Miners set up their own courts of law.
- In 1853, San Francisco had 537 saloons.

Student answer

In 1849, gold was discovered in California and so the gold rush began. Thousands of miners travelled west. Around 90,000 single men arrived in California from all parts of the world. They argued and fought each other over claims and over gold. In the towns that grew up, miners regularly got drunk, went with prostitutes and had drunken brawls. San Francisco had more than 500 saloons. Some mining towns set up their own law courts but the justice they handed out was a bit rough and ready.

Examiner comments

This candidate has written a description of life in the early mining towns and has added to the information given in the question. The answer has picked out the problems of law and order. In order to improve the answer and gain more marks, the candidate should focus more strongly on giving a clear explanation of why a range of problems arose, rather than simply describing them.

Extract from an improved student answer

Problems like these were caused because the early mining towns grew so quickly and because there were violent people in them. The chance of making a quick fortune attracted criminals who came to prey on those miners lucky enough to strike gold. Additionally, since most miners were single men, there wasn't the civilising influence of women and children. The first settlements had no structure and no proper system of town government to organise law and order. The only law to start with was force. Gunmen imposed their own law, their own courts and their own system of punishment. That added to the violence and disorder. The main cause of the problems was distance – from organised government, from law officers and from civilised society.

How important were the railroads in destroying the traditional life of the Plains Indians after 1867? (16 marks)

You may use the following in your answer and any other information of your own.

- The government gave the railroad companies 17 million acres of land in the years 1865 to 1871.
- In the years 1872 to 1874, almost 14 million buffalo hides were sent to the east of the United States.
- In 1874, gold was discovered in the Black Hills.

Student answer

The destruction of the way of life of the Plains Indians began when the government gave the railroad companies 17 million acres of land in the years 1865 to 1871. This was all part of the government's cunning 'manifest destiny' plan whereby the whole of America had to be peopled by white Americans. The railroad pushed through the Indians' hunting grounds, frightening the buffalo. The railroads also brought buffalo killers on to the Plains and millions of buffalo hides were sent back by railroad to the east of the USA. The Indians' way of life depended on the buffalo. Without them they had to depend on handouts in reservations.

Examiner comments

This response describes two ways in which the Plains Indians' way of life was destroyed: by crossing their hunting grounds and by destroying the buffalo. Some linkage is made between the railroads and the destruction of the Plains Indians' way of life. To improve the answer the student should:

- make clearer the links between the railroad and the life of the Plains Indians
- consider other ways the railroads affected the Plains Indians
- consider other factors that helped destroy the Plains Indians' way of life
- reach a judgment about which factor was most important.

Improved student answer

Miners, settlers and ranchers all wanted to use areas that Plains Indians had once been able to use freely. The railroads were one factor in the destruction of the Indian way of life, because they created competition for that land. The development of the cattle industry only happened because of the railroads that could take thousands of carcasses to the eastern states. The railroads brought homesteaders on to the Plains as well as all the supplies they needed. They brought buffalo hunters who destroyed the herds the Indians depended on.

But other factors were important. The discovery of gold in the Black Hills led to the breaking of treaties guaranteeing the Black Hills to the Sioux and to conflict between the army and the Plains Indians when army forts were built in Indian territory to protect routes to the gold [student adds examples].

The most important reason was the role of the US government, which combined all the factors. In order to fulfil the idea of 'manifest destiny', it brushed aside the protests of the Indians that treaties were being broken [student adds examples] and it supported the expansion of railroads by giving them free land. It directed the role of the army, which was a big factor in defeating the Indians, at the Battle of Wounded Knee for example. The government forced Indians into reservations, took away their skills and tried to turn them into farmers in order to free up the Plains for settlement by homesteaders and ranchers.

Don't Panic Zone

As you get close to completing your revision, the Big Day will be getting nearer and nearer. Many students find this the most stressful time and tend to go into panic mode, either working long hours without really giving their brains a chance to absorb information, or giving up and staring blankly at the wall.

Panicking simply makes your brain seize up and you find that information and thoughts simply cannot flow naturally. You become distracted and anxious, and things seem worse than they are. Many students build the exams up into more than they are. Remember: the exams are not trying to catch you out! If you have studied the course, there will be no surprises on the exam paper!

Student tip

I know how silly it is to panic, especially if you've done the work and know your stuff. I was asked by a teacher to produce a report on a project I'd done, and I panicked so much I spent the whole afternoon crying and worrying. I asked other people for help, but they were panicking, too. In the end, I calmed down and looked at the task again. It turned out to be quite straightforward and, in the end, I got my report finished first and it was the best of them all!

In the exam you don't have much time, so you can't waste it by panicking. The best way to control panic is simply to do what you have to do. Think carefully for a few minutes, then start writing and, as you do, the panic will drain away.

Don't panic

Exam Zone

You will have an hour and a quarter for this exam paper and in that time you have to answer four questions. You need to answer Questions 1 and 2. Then you must choose to answer one question from Questions 3 and 4, and then choose to answer one question from Questions 5 and 6.

Each question is worth a different amount of marks and it is important that you use your time effectively. Don't waste precious time on a 4-mark question that might then leave you with too little time to spend on a question which is worth 16 marks!

Meet the exam paper

This diagram shows the front cover of the exam paper. These instructions, information and advice will always appear on the front of the paper. It is worth reading it carefully now. Check you understand it. Now is a good opportunity to ask your teacher about anything you are not sure of here.

109

Print your surname here, and your other names afterwards. This is an additional safeguard to ensure that the exam board awards the marks to the right candicate.

Here you fill in the school's exam number.

Ensure that you understand exactly how long the examination will last, and plan your time accordingly.

Note that the quality of your written communication will also be marked. Take particular care to present your thoughts and work at the highest standard you can, for maximum marks.

Here you fill in your personal exam number. Take care when writing it down because the number is important to the exam board when writing your score.

In this box, the examiner will write the total marks you have achieved in the exam paper.

Make sure that you understand exactly which questions from which sections you should attempt.

Don't feel that you have to fill the answer space provided. Everybody's handwriting varies, so a long answer from you may take up as much space as a short answer from someone else.

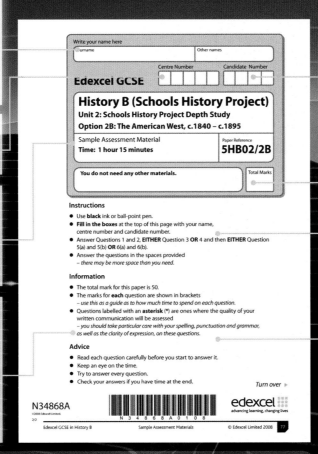

Understanding the language of the exam paper

Describe	The examiner is looking for a concise and organised account. Jot down three or four points in the margin that you want to include in your answer. Arrange them in the most logical order.
Explain how	The examiner is trying to discover whether you understand the key events in the American West c1840–c1895, and why they happened. The more detail you can give, the more marks you will receive.
Give reasons for your answer	You need to provide an explanation.
How far	The examiner is looking for points for and against the statement. Make sure you find some on both sides.
Do you agree?	You are free to agree or disagree. What makes a difference is how well you back up your case.

Zone Out

This section provides answers to the most common questions students have about what happens after they complete their exams. For much more information, visit www.heinemann.co.uk/hotlinks (express code 4431P) and click on 'ExamZone'.

About your grades

Whether you've done better than, worse than or just as you expected, your grades are the final measure of your performance on your course and in the exams. On this page we explain some of the information that appears on your results slip and tell you what to do if you think something is wrong. We answer the most popular questions about grades and look at some of the options facing you.

When will my results be published?

Results are issued on the **middle** two Thursdays in August with GCE first and GCSE second.

Can I get my results online?

Visit www.heinemann.co.uk/hotlinks (express code 4431P) and click on 'ResultsPlus', where you will find detailed student results information including the 'Edexcel Gradeometer', which demonstrates how close you were to the nearest grade boundary. You will need a password to access this information, which can be retrieved from your school's exam secretary

I haven't done as well as I expected. What can I do now?

First of all, talk to your subject teacher. After all the teaching, tests and internal examinations that you have had, he/she is the person who best knows what grade you are capable of achieving. Take your results slip to your subject teacher, and go through the information on it in detail. If you both think that there is something wrong with the result, the school or college can apply to see your completed examination paper and then, if necessary, ask for a re-mark immediately. The original mark can be confirmed or lowered, as well as raised, as a result of a re-mark.

How do my grades compare with those of everybody else who sat this exam?

You can compare your results with those of others in the UK who have completed the same examination using the information on the Edexcel website accessed at www.heinemann.co.uk/hotlinks (express code 4431P) by clicking on 'Edexcel'.

I achieved a higher mark for the same unit last time. Can I use that result?

Yes. The higher score is the one that goes towards your overall grade. Even if you sat a unit more than twice, the best result will be used automatically when the overall grade is calculated. You do not need to ask us to take into account a previous result. This will be done automatically, so you can be assured that all your best unit results have gone into calculating your overall grade.

What happens if I was ill over the period of my examinations?

If you become ill before or during the examination period you are eligible for special consideration. This also applies if you have been affected by an accident, bereavement or serious disturbance during an examination.

If my school has requested special consideration for me, is this shown on my Statement of Results?

If your school has requested special consideration for you, it is not shown on your results slip, but it will be shown on a subject mark report that is sent to your school or college. If you want to know whether special consideration was requested for you, you should ask your Examinations Officer.

Can I have a re-mark of my examination paper?

Yes, this is possible, but remember that only your school or college can apply for a re-mark, not you or your parents/carers. First of all, you should consider carefully whether or not to ask your school or college to make a request for a re-mark. You should remember that very few re-marks result in a change to a grade – not because Edexcel is embarrassed that a change of marks has been made, but simply because a re-mark request has shown that the original marking was accurate. Check the closing date for re-marking requests with your Examinations Officer.

When I asked for a re-mark of my paper, my subject grade went down. What can I do?

There is no guarantee that your grades will go up if your papers are re-marked. They can also go down or stay the same. After a re-mark, the only way to improve your grade is to take the examination again. Your school or college Examinations Officer can tell you when you can do that.

How many times can I resit a unit?

You can resit a unit from your History B course once and the best result for each unit in the course will then count towards the final grade. If you have finished all your assessments for the course and then decide you want to resit a unit, you have to do a minimum of 40 per cent of the assessments again in your resit.

For much more information, go to www.heinemann.co.uk/hotlinks (express code 4431P) and click on 'Examzone'.

Glossary

breech-loading rifle – a rifle that loads at the breech, where the gun breaks

cattle drover – a cowboy who herded cattle along the trails
chuck wagon – a wagon where cowboys kept food and cooking utensils while travelling the trails
claim – an amount of land registered by a homesteader or miner for his own use
claim-jumping – stealing another person's claim to prospect for gold in a specific place
corral – an enclosure for cattle or horses
counting coup – the act of touching an enemy

Danites – Mormon secret police
dry farming – a technique whereby farmers ploughed their land whenever it rained or snowed, thus creating a layer of dust that trapped the moisture underneath

federal – relating to a government that makes laws for all the United States

Gatling gun – an early machine gun that could fire rapidly
Ghost Dance – an Indian dance that was believed to bring all dead Indians to life in order to have a final battle with the white man

homesteader – a person who settled on the Great Plains to farm the land
Hotchkiss cannon – a cannon that fired rapidly and was light enough to be used with cavalry

Indian agent – an Indian appointed by the government to help run the reservations

jerky – strips of dried buffalo meat

lodge – sometimes used as an alternative name for a tipi, or for a collection of tipis
lynching – hanging without trial

manifest destiny – the belief that white Americans should populate the United States from east to west coast
marshal – a man appointed by the US President to be responsible for law and order in a state or territory
medicine man – Indian holy man
mountain man – a man who was a hunter, trapper and tracker in the Rocky Mountains
muzzle-loading rifle – a rifle that is loaded down through its muzzle

nomadic – moving around from place to place

pemmican – buffalo meat that has been pounded to a pulp, mixed with berries, poured into a skin container and sealed with fat
polygamy – having more than one wife at the same time
pony express – a rider on a fast pony who carried mail across the Plains before the railroads
posse van – a coach full of armed guards attached to a train
primary settlement – the first, most basic settlement

railhead – a station where cattle were picked up for transporting to the eastern states
reservation – an area designated for Indian use
riding shotgun – armed men riding on a stagecoach to protect it from attack
road agent – highwayman
rustling – stealing animals that were part of a herd

sacred land – holy land
scalping – cutting away the hair and scalp of a defeated enemy as a trophy of battle
scout – an Indian or a soldier sent ahead of the main party to find out the lie of the land
sheriff – a lawman appointed, usually for two-year periods, to be responsible for law and order in a county
sod-buster – another name for a homesteader
sod house – houses built from sods of earth by homesteaders
speculator – person who bought land intending to sell it on at a higher price
subsidy – help given in goods or money
sweat lodge – a tipi where the air is heated inside and people go to sweat as part of a purification ritual

tannery – a factory where buffalo skins were made into leather
teetotaller – a person who does not drink alcohol
tipi – a tent-like home of an Indian family
total war – war in which everyone is involved – civilians as well as combatants
trading station – the place where mountain men, Indians and traders met to buy and sell furs, skins and other goods
travois – framework harnessed to a horse on which Plains Indians transported their belongings

vigilante – member of a community that took the law into their own hands
vision – a person or object seen in a dream or a trance

warpath – hunting down an enemy
watershed – a ridge or high piece of land from which water flows in two different directions

Index

In the following index, main entries of key words are given in **bold** type and the page number that is also in bold will lead you to a definition of the word. These definitions can also be found in the Glossary on page 112.

Index